Glencoe

WORLD HISTORY

Unit 2 Resources

Glencoe McGraw-Hill

New York, New York   Columbus, Ohio   Chicago, Illinois   Peoria, Illinois   Woodland Hills, California

Book Organization

Glencoe offers resources that accompany *Glencoe World History* to expand, enrich, review, and assess every lesson you teach and for every student you teach.

HOW THIS BOOK IS ORGANIZED

Each Unit Resources book offers blackline masters at unit, chapter, and section levels. Each book is divided into three parts—unit-based resources, chapter-based resources, and section-based resources. Tabs facilitate navigation.

UNIT-BASED RESOURCES

We have organized this book so that all unit resources appear at the beginning. Although you may choose to use the specific activities at any time during the course of unit study, Glencoe has placed these resources up front so that you can review your options. For example, the Economics and History Activities and World Literature Readings appear in the front of this book, but you may plan to use these resources in class at any time during the study of the unit.

CHAPTER-BASED AND SECTION-BASED RESOURCES

Chapter-based resources follow the unit materials. For example, Chapter 6 blackline masters appear in this book immediately following Unit 2 materials. The materials appear in the order you teach—Chapter 6 activities; Chapter 6 section activities; Chapter 7 activities; Chapter 7 section activities; and so on.

A COMPLETE ANSWER KEY

A complete answer key appears at the back of this book. This answer key includes answers for all activities in this book in the order in which the activities appear.

Glencoe/McGraw-Hill

A Division of The **McGraw·Hill** Companies

Send all inquiries to:
Glencoe/McGraw-Hill
8787 Orion Place
Columbus, Ohio 43240-4027

ISBN 0-07-829434-7

Printed in the United States of America

1 2 3 4 5 6 7 8 9 10   009   08 07 06 05 04 03 02

Table of Contents

To the Teacher

Glencoe's Unit Resources books offer varied activities to enhance the learning experience of your students.

Charting and Graphing Activities
Students organize information in either a chart or graph. These activities are designed to help students learn visually and to stimulate critical thinking abilities.

Economics and History Activities
These readings give students a greater understanding of the impact of economics on history and familiarize students with economic terms and principles. Each reading is followed by comprehension and critical thinking questions and activities.

World Literature Readings
Students read literature from some of the time periods and cultures covered by the textbook. Each selection is preceded by background information and a guided reading suggestion and is followed by comprehension and critical thinking questions.

Vocabulary Activities
These review-and-reinforcement activities help students master unfamiliar terms used in the textbook. The worksheets emphasize identification of word meanings and provide visual and kinesthetic reinforcement of language skills.

Skills Reinforcement Activities
These activities are designed to introduce and reinforce important social studies, critical thinking, technology, study, and writing skills.

Critical Thinking Skills Activities
These activities show students how to use information to make judgments, develop their own ideas, and apply what they have learned to new situations.

History and Geography Activities
Students analyze and interpret maps in relation to historical events. Students use geography skills as an aid to understanding history.

Mapping History Activities
Each activity helps students develop and practice map-based skills by analyzing and interpreting a map. The content and exercises are related to the textbook.

Historical Significance Activities
These activities relate some aspect of a time period from the textbook to something in the present day. Students see how codes of law, institutions, customs, and concerns from the past are with us today.

Cooperative Learning Activities
These extension activities offer students clear directions for working together on a variety of activities that enrich prior learning.

History Simulation Activities
Students work in small groups to explore a theme, topic, or concept from the textbook. Many of these activities use a game or simulation format to stimulate student interest. Groups document their efforts by completing a chart, diagram, or planning sheet.

Time Line Activities
These activities are designed to reinforce the dates of major events in world history and to help students learn the chronological order of those events. Each activity includes a time line labeled with events and dates. Students answer questions based on the time line.

Linking Past and Present Activities
Students analyze readings that describe past and present ideas, customs, art, architecture, scientific breakthroughs, and governments. Students learn that individuals, societies, and cultures continue to grapple with many of the same issues.

People in World History Profiles
These biographical sketches of significant figures from world history expose students to a diversity of cultures and time periods. Questions emphasize the role of individuals in historical events.

Primary Source Readings
Students study the original written works of people throughout history. Each selection is preceded by an introduction and a guided reading suggestion and is followed by questions that allow students to analyze and interpret the material.

Reteaching Activities
These varied activities enable students to visualize the connections among facts in their textbook. Graphs, charts, tables, and concept maps are among the many types of graphic organizers used.

Enrichment Activities
These activities introduce content that is different from, but related to, the themes, ideas, and information in the textbook. Students develop a broader and deeper understanding of the relationship of historical events to the contemporary world.

World Art and Music Activities
Students are exposed to art and music from around the world. Critical thinking questions help students to understand art and music within a historical context.

Guided Reading Activities
These activities provide help for students who are having difficulty comprehending the text. Students fill in information in the guided reading outlines, sentence completion activities, or other information-organizing exercises as they read the textbook.

Glencoe

Unit 2 Resources

New Patterns of Civilization: 400–1500

Charting and Graphing Activity 2

Diversity of Rulers

Directions: Rulers of kingdoms and dynasties in Africa and Asia possessed many powers that they used in a variety of ways. The chart below identifies several of these leaders and their dynasties. Complete the chart by adding a description of the nature of each leader's rule.

African and Asian Rulers		
Ruler	**Dynasty or Kingdom**	**Nature of Rule**
Mansa Musa	**kingdom of Mali**	
Sunni Ali	**Sunni dynasty**	
Harun al-Rashid	**Abbasid dynasty**	
Sui Yangdi	**Sui dynasty**	
Tang Xuanzang	**Tang dynasty**	
Kublai Khan	**Mongol dynasty**	
Minamoto Yoritomo	**Kamakura shogunate**	

Economics and History Activity 2

The Growth of Cities

One of the key factors that contributed to the growth of cities was the development of more advanced farming tools and techniques. These tools and techniques enabled fewer farmers to grow greater amounts of food, thus freeing other people to pursue different careers. Once large cities had begun to grow, there were also other significant factors that contributed to the success and development of cities.

One such factor was "international" trade, a practice whereby people began to exchange goods with other groups or cities that were outside their own societal or cultural groups. International trade brought about changes in local economies. Businesses now had the additional task of competing with businesses that were outside the local economy. Businesses also began to have additional sources of revenue—the income or goods they earned through trading with people who lived outside their own societal or cultural groups. Businesses that produced goods that were in great demand in foreign markets could succeed even when their local economies faced hard times.

The Silk Road One important trade route that existed long ago was the Silk Road. This major trade route stretched from Venice, Italy, to what is now Beijing, China. The Silk Road passed through ports on the Mediterranean Sea and along roads throughout Europe, the Middle East, and Asia. The Silk Road was used for travel and trade as early as 200 B.C. However, the collapse of the Roman Empire and China's Han dynasty led to a decline in trade along the Silk Road.

In the 1300s, the Silk Road again became a major trading route, habituated by traders in camel convoys and on ships. The average Egyptian who wanted (and could afford) to purchase tea from China did not actually travel the Silk Road in order to acquire the tea. Instead, that Egyptian would buy the tea from a trading company, which was comprised of many individual traders, each of whom was responsible for a different segment of the Silk Road. As the demand for foreign products increased throughout Europe, North Africa, and Asia, trading along the Silk Road also increased, and the trading companies prospered.

The Banking System As international trade continued to flourish, banking firms also expanded. Bank-like operations had been around since the Middle Ages, when people

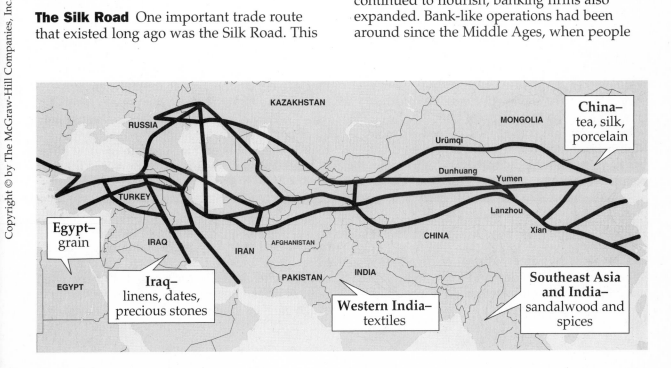

UNIT 2

Economics and History Activity 2

had begun to use the safes of goldsmiths to protect their money. When people deposited their money in the safes, the goldsmiths gave them a receipt for that money. Over time, people began to use those receipts as a form of currency. Technically, the goldsmiths were not yet bankers; in actuality they functioned merely as storage houses. Eventually, however, goldsmiths began lending the coins that other people had left with them—and charging interest on these loans. Goldsmiths felt secure lending out other people's coins, knowing that not everyone would withdraw all of their money at once. The goldsmiths had become bankers—people who earned interest by lending other people's money.

The need for proper record keeping became critical as the banking and trading industries grew. Record keepers, or bookkeepers as they became known, tracked inventory, shipments, and payments. Businesses needed better-educated workers to provide these services in order to assure that their accounts were in order. These workers became part of the emerging merchant class.

The new merchant class was born out of the wealth created by the economic boom that took place in many of the major cities along the Silk Road. The new class of people would become the foundation of a group known as the middle class. Members of the middle class were neither royalty nor wealthy, nor were they peasants or slaves. Instead, the middle class was a growing group of people who were free and, in some cases, owned property. Members of the middle class, however, did not have the same power that the extremely wealthy or royal families of that time had. Still, the wealth that the middle class possessed did give them a certain level of prestige. As the middle class grew, so too did their power.

The growth of international trade resulted in an increase in the demand for gold and silver coins. These coins were used to purchase goods along the Silk Road.

A Developing Money Economy A trading company could not expect a merchant in China to accept the medium of exchange used in France. Due to this, a money economy, or an economic system based on money rather than barter, slowly began to develop. At first the type of money used was typically gold and silver coins. Much like other mediums of exchange, gold and silver coins had value in and of themselves—the precious metals that made up the coin had actual purchasing power; paper money has no intrinsic value. For this reason, banks and governments backed their currency (paper money and coins) with silver. This meant that people could actually exchange their paper money for specific amounts of silver. In 1821, Great Britain began using a gold standard for its money. Over the next 50 years, many countries followed suit.

World War I brought about an end to the international gold standard. Although some countries reintroduced it again after the war, the Great Depression of the 1930s brought a virtual end to this monetary policy.

Today the money supply is made up of currency and demand deposits. Demand deposits are checking deposits. It is not the check itself that is considered money. In fact, a check is a worthless piece of paper unless it is deposited or cashed at a bank.

Most countries today use their own currency to conduct business within their economy. In the United States, the paper currency says "Federal Reserve Note." This means that all paper currency is issued to banks by the United States Federal Reserve. In other words, the U.S. Federal Reserve is responsible for regulating how much money is placed in circulation. The United States Treasury, however, prints the actual bills.

How can people trade internationally if there are so many different currencies? People trade currencies so that they will have the appropriate currency for a given country. The rate of exchange, or exchange rate, tells how much each currency is worth in relation to the

Economics and History Activity 2

UNIT 2

other. For example, one U.S. dollar might be worth 120 Japanese yen. Exchange rates are determined by many factors. The value of one country's money in comparison to another country's money changes over time. At any given time, the exchange rate is generally agreed upon. However, as people who travel have discovered, a person may receive a different rate of exchange depending upon where he or she trades the money.

Applying Economics to History

Directions: Use the information you have read and the diagrams to answer the following questions on a separate sheet of paper.

Recalling Information
1. Explain the importance of exchange rates.
2. What was the Silk Road?
3. How did the Silk Road lead to the development of trading companies and to an increase in banking firms?
4. Describe the merchant class. How were merchants different from the other classes of people?

Critical Thinking
5. **Making Inferences** Why are education and the use of writing so important in the growth of trading economies?
6. **Analyzing Information** Explain why a goldsmith was not a banker.

Making Connections
7. The following table shows the exchange rate for several countries. Choose one of

these countries and determine the cost in its currency for a pair of jeans, lunch at your favorite restaurant, and a movie ticket. (Note: Each country's currency is based on the U.S. dollar. For example 715 pesos is equal to one U.S. dollar.)

Exchange Rate for Selected Countries

Country	Exchange Rate	Name of Currency
United States	1.00	dollar
Canada	1.56	dollar
Chile	715.00	peso
Japan	120.91	yen
Russia	30.00	ruble

8. Work with a small group or a partner to complete the following research project: Think about the many products that you buy, such as clothing, food, and games. Choose one product and create a chart or diagram showing the route taken by that product to your home. Consider where the product was manufactured, the port or city at which it entered the United States, and the store where you bought it. If the product was made in the United States, it still may have made many stops within the country before arriving in your home.

World Literature Reading 2

The Thousand and One Nights is a collection of stories linked by a single frame tale. King Shahrayar marries a different woman each night and puts her to death the next morning. To delay her death, one wife, Princess Shahrazad (sometimes spelled Scheherazade), tells the king a story each night but withholds the ending until the following day. The tales continue for a thousand and one nights, a total of almost three years. By that time, King Shahrayar has fallen in love with Princess Shahrazad and decides not to have her killed.

The Thousand and One Nights is based on the *Hazar Afsanah*, an ancient Persian collection of stories likely written by many different people. The book was translated into Arabic around 850 B.C. and renamed *The Thousand and One Nights*.

GUIDED READING As you read "The Story of the Merchant and the Demon" and "The Fisherman and the Jinnee," think about what lesson each story teaches.

from *The Thousand and One Nights*

The Story of the Merchant and the Demon

It is said, O wise and happy King, that once there was a prosperous merchant who had abundant wealth and investments and commitments in every country. He had many women and children and kept many servants and slaves. One day, having resolved to visit another country, he took provisions, filling his saddlebag with loaves of bread and with dates, mounted his horse, and set out on his journey. For many days and nights, he journeyed under God's care until he reached his destination. When he finished his business, he turned back to his home and family. He journeyed for three days, and on the fourth day, chancing to come to an orchard, went in to avoid the heat and shade himself from the sun of the open country. He came to a spring under a walnut tree and, tying his horse, sat by the spring, pulled out from the saddlebag some loaves of bread and a handful of dates, and began to eat, throwing the date pits right and left until he had had enough. Then he got up, performed his ablutions, and performed his prayers.

But hardly had he finished when he saw an old demon, with sword in hand, standing with his feet on the ground and his head in the clouds. The demon approached until he stood before him and screamed, saying, "Get up, so that I may kill you with this sword, just as you have killed my son."

When the merchant saw and heard the demon, he was terrified and awestricken. He asked, "Master, for what crime do you wish to kill me?"

The demon replied, "I wish to kill you because you have killed my son."

The merchant asked, "Who has killed your son?"

The demon replied, "You have killed my son."

World Literature Reading 2

From *The Thousand and One Nights* (continued)

The merchant said, "By God, I did not kill your son. When and how could that have been?"

The demon said, "Didn't you sit down, take out some dates from your saddlebag, and eat, throwing the pits right and left?"

The merchant replied, "Yes, I did."

The demon said, "You killed my son, for as you were throwing the stones right and left, my son happened to be walking by and was struck and killed by one of them, and I must now kill you."

The merchant said, "O my lord, please don't kill me."

The demon replied, "I must kill you as you killed him—blood for blood."

The merchant said, "To God we belong and to God we turn. There is no power or strength, save in God the Almighty, the Magnificent. If I killed him, I did it by mistake. Please forgive me."

The demon replied, "By God, I must kill you, as you killed my son." Then he seized him, and throwing him to the ground, raised the sword to strike him.

The merchant began to weep and mourn his family and his wife and children. Again, the demon raised his sword to strike, while the merchant cried until he was drenched with tears, saying, "There is no power or strength, save in God the Almighty, the Magnificent." Then he began to recite the following verses:

Life has two days: one peace, one
    wariness,
And has two sides: worry and happiness.
Ask him who taunts us with adversity,
"Does fate, save those worthy of note,
    oppress?
Don't you see that the blowing, raging
    storms
Only the tallest of the trees beset,
And of earth's many green and barren
    lots,
Only the ones with fruits with stones are
    hit,
And of the countless stars in heaven's
    vault
None is eclipsed except the moon and
    sun?
You thought well of the days, when they
    were good,
Oblivious to the ills destined for one.
You were deluded by the peaceful
    nights,
Yet in the peace of night does sorrow
    stun."

When the merchant finished and stopped weeping, the demon said, "By God, I must kill you, as you killed my son, even if you weep blood."

The merchant asked, "Must you?"

The demon replied, "I must," and raised his sword to strike.

But morning overtook Shahrazad, and she lapsed into silence, leaving King Shahrayar burning with curiosity to hear the rest of the story. Then Dinarzad said to her sister Shahrazad, "What a strange and lovely story!"

Shahrazad replied, "What is this compared with what I shall tell you tomorrow night if the king spares me and lets me live? It will be even better and more entertaining."

The king thought to himself, "I will spare her until I hear the rest of the story; then I will have her put to death the next day."

When morning broke, the day dawned, and the sun rose; the king left to attend to the affairs of the kingdom, and the vizier, Shahrazad's father, was amazed and delighted. King Shahrayar governed all day and returned home at night to his quarters. . . . Then Dinarzad said to her sister Shahrazad, "Please, sister, if you are not sleepy, tell us one of your lovely little tales to while away the night."

The king added, "Let it be the conclusion of the story of the demon and the merchant, for I would like to hear it."

World Literature Reading 2

From *The Thousand and One Nights* (continued)

Copyright © by The McGraw-Hill Companies, Inc.

Shahrazad replied, "With the greatest pleasure, dear, happy King."

The following night, Shahrazad completes the story. Then she begins a new story for the king, but day breaks before she can finish it, so the king spares her life for another night. The following is another of the stories Shahrazad tells during her ordeal.

The Fisherman and the Jinnee

Once upon a time there was a poor fisherman who had a wife and three children to support.

He used to cast his net four times a day. It chanced that one day he went down to the sea at noon and, reaching the shore, set down his basket, rolled up his shirt-sleeves, and cast his net far out into the water. After he had waited for it to sink, he pulled on the cords with all his might; but the net was so heavy that he could not draw it in. So he tied the rope ends to a wooden stake on the beach and, putting off his clothes, dived into the water and set to work to bring it up. When he had carried it ashore, he found in it a dead donkey.

"By Allah, this is a strange catch!" cried the fisherman, disgusted at the sight. After he had freed the net and wrung it out, he waded into the water and cast it again, invoking Allah's help. But when he tried to draw it in he found it even heavier than before. Thinking that he had caught some enormous fish, he fastened the ropes to the stake and, diving in again, brought up the net. This time he found a large earthen vessel filled with mud and sand.

Angrily the fisherman threw away the vessel, cleaned his net, and cast it for the third time. He waited patiently, and when he felt the net grow heavy he hauled it in, only to find it filled with bones and broken glass. In despair, he lifted his eyes to heaven and cried: "Allah knows that I cast my net only four times a day. I have already cast it for the third time and caught no fish at all. Surely He will not fail me again!"

With this the fisherman hurled his net far out into the sea, and waited for it to sink to the bottom. When at length he brought it to land he found in it a bottle made of yellow copper. The mouth was stopped with lead and bore the seal of our master Solomon son of David. The fisherman rejoiced, and said: "I will sell this in the market of the coppersmiths. It must be worth ten pieces of gold." He shook the bottle and, finding it heavy, thought to himself: "I will first break the seal and find out what is inside."

The fisherman removed the lead with his knife and again shook the bottle; but scarcely had he done so, when there burst from it a great column of smoke which spread along the shore and rose so high that it almost touched the heavens. Taking shape, the smoke resolved itself into a jinnee of such prodigious stature that his head reached the clouds, while his feet were planted on the sand. His head was a huge dome and his mouth as wide as a cavern, with teeth ragged like broken rocks. His legs towered like the masts of a ship, his nostrils were two inverted bowls, and his eyes, blazing like torches, made his aspect fierce and menacing.

World Literature Reading 2

From *The Thousand and One Nights* (continued)

The sight of this jinnee struck terror to the fisherman's heart; his limbs quivered, his teeth chattered together, and he stood rooted to the ground with parched tongue and staring eyes.

"There is no god but Allah and Solomon is His Prophet!" cried the jinnee. Then, addressing himself to the fisherman, he said: "I pray you, mighty Prophet, do not kill me! I swear never again to defy your will or violate your laws!"

"Blasphemous giant," cried the fisherman, "do you presume to call Solomon the Prophet of Allah? Solomon has been dead these eighteen hundred years, and we are approaching the end of Time. But what is your history, pray, and how came you to be imprisoned in this bottle?"

On hearing these words the jinnee replied sarcastically: "Well, then; there is no god but Allah! Fisherman, I bring you good news."

"What news?" asked the old man.

"News of your death, horrible and prompt!" replied the jinnee.

"Then may heaven's wrath be upon you, ungrateful wretch!" cried the fisherman. "Why do you wish my death, and what have I done to deserve it? Have I not brought you up from the depths of the sea and released you from your imprisonment?"

But the jinnee answered: "Choose the manner of your death and the way I shall kill you. Come, waste no time!"

"But what crime have I committed?" cried the fisherman.

"Listen to my story, and you shall know," replied the jinnee.

"Be brief, then, I pray you," said the fisherman, "for you have wrung my soul with terror."

"Know," began the giant, "that I am one of the rebel jinn who, together with Sakhr the Jinnee, mutinied against Solomon son of David. Solomon sent against me his Vizier, Asaf ben Berakhya, who vanquished me despite my supernatural power and led me captive before his master. Invoking the name of Allah, Solomon adjured me to embrace his faith and pledge him absolute obedience. I refused, and he imprisoned me in this bottle, upon which he set a seal of lead bearing the Name of the Most High. Then he sent for several of his faithful jinn, who carried me away and cast me into the middle of the sea. In the ocean depths I vowed: 'I will bestow eternal riches on him who sets me free!' But a hundred years passed away and no one freed me. In the second hundred years of my imprisonment I said: 'For him who frees me I will open up the buried treasures of the earth!' And yet no one freed me. Whereupon I flew into a rage and swore: 'I will kill the man who sets me free, allowing him only to choose the manner of his death!' Now it was you who set me free; therefore prepare to die and choose the way that I shall kill you."

"O wretched luck, that it should have fallen to my lot to free you!" exclaimed the fisherman. "Spare me, mighty jinnee, and Allah will spare you; kill me, and so shall Allah destroy you!"

"You have freed me," repeated the jinnee. "Therefore you must die."

"Chief of the jinn," cried the fisherman, "will you thus requite good with evil?"

"Enough of this talk!" roared the jinnee. "Kill you I must."

At this point the fisherman thought to himself: "Though I am but a man and he is a jinnee, my cunning may yet overreach his malice." Then, turning to his adversary, he said: "Before you kill me, I beg you in the Name of the Most High engraved on Solomon's seal to answer me one question truthfully."

World Literature Reading 2

From *The Thousand and One Nights* (continued)

The jinnee trembled at the mention of the Name, and, when he had promised to answer truthfully, the fisherman asked: "How could this bottle, which is scarcely large enough to hold your hand or foot, ever contain your entire body?"

"Do you dare doubt that?" roared the jinnee indignantly.

"I will never believe it," replied the fisherman, "until I see you enter this bottle with my own eyes!"

Upon this the jinnee trembled from head to foot and dissolved into a column of smoke, which gradually wound itself into the bottle and disappeared inside. At once the fisherman snatched up the leaden stopper and thrust it into the mouth of the bottle. Then he called out to the jinnee: "Choose the manner of your death and the way that I shall kill you! By Allah, I will throw you back into the sea, and keep watch on this shore to warn all men of your treachery!"

When he heard the fisherman's words, the jinnee struggled desperately to escape from the bottle, but was prevented by the magic seal. He now altered his tone and, assuming a submissive air, assured the fisherman that he had been jesting with him and implored him to let him out. But the fisherman paid no heed to the jinnee's entreaties, and resolutely carried the bottle down to the sea.

"What are you doing to me?" whimpered the jinnee helplessly.

"I am going to throw you back into the sea!" replied the fisherman. "You have lain in the depths eighteen hundred years, and there you shall remain till the Last Judgement! Did I not beg you to spare me so that Allah might spare you? But you took no pity on me, and He has now delivered you into my hands." . . .

"Let me out! Let me out!" cried the jinnee in despair. "I will never harm you, and promise to render you a service that will enrich you!"

At length the fisherman accepted the jinee's pledge, and after he had made him swear by the Most High Name, opened the bottle with trembling hands.

World Literature Reading 2

From *The Thousand and One Nights* (continued)

DIRECTIONS: Answer the following questions in the space provided.

Interpreting the Reading

1. How would you describe Shahrazad, based on her actions while telling "The Story of the Merchant and the Demon"?

_____

_____

_____

2. In "The Fisherman and the Jinnee," what character flaw does the jinnee have that allows the fisherman to outsmart him?

_____

_____

_____

3. What is the moral theme that these two stories share?

_____

_____

_____

Critical Thinking

4. Making Predictions How do you think "The Story of the Merchant and the Demon" ends?

_____

_____

_____

5. Making Comparisons "The Story of the Merchant and the Demon" and "The Fisherman and the Jinnee" are just two of the 1,001 tales Shahrazad tells the king in an effort to delay her death. How do the situations described in these two stories relate to Shahrazad's situation?

_____

_____

_____

_____

Chapter 6 Resources
The World of Islam, 600–1500

♪B♪C Vocabulary Activity 6

The World of Islam, 600–1500

DIRECTIONS: Select and write the term that best completes each sentence.

• sheikh	• angel	• *shari'ah*
• mosque	• Islam	• hajj
• caliph	• jihad	• *Hijrah*
• bazaar	• dowry	• arabesque
• chronicle	• Quran	• sultan

1. The voice Muhammad heard calling him to be the apostle of Allah was that of an

   _____.

2. The _____ is the journey made by Muhammad and his followers to Madinah.

3. The commercial center of towns where goods were sold was called the

   _____.

4. A Bedouin tribal chieftain was a _____.

5. The pilgrimage to Makkah is the _____.

6. A narrative of events in the order in which they occurred is a _____.

7. The leader of the Islamic civilization is a _____.

8. The Muslim code of law is the _____.

9. Money or property brought by a groom to his wife at marriage is called a

   _____.

10. A Muslim house of worship is a _____.

11. Arabic script entwined with plant stems and geometric designs is an

    _____.

12. _____ means submission to the will of Allah.

13. A struggle or conflict to spread Islam is a _____.

14. The book containing the ethical guidelines and laws followed by Muslims is known as the _____.

15. _____ is a Turkish title that describes someone who holds power.

Skills Reinforcement Activity 6

Taking Notes

Effective note taking involves breaking up much of the information you read or hear into meaningful parts so that you can understand and remember it. As you listen or read, take note of key points that are emphasized. In written material, look for topic sentences and words in bold or italic type. Clues like these will help you identify important concepts. Your notes should be neatly written and should summarize in your own words the main ideas and supporting details of your subject.

Directions: Read about Islamic culture on pages 207–210 of your textbook. Fill in the missing information in the outline below to prepare notes.

Main Idea: Philosophy, Science, and History

1. _____

2. _____

3. _____

4. _____

Main Idea: Literature

1. _____

2. _____

3. _____

4. _____

Main Idea: Art and Architecture

1. _____

2. _____

3. _____

4. _____

CHAPTER 6

Critical Thinking Skills Activity 6 | Recognizing Ideologies

An ideology is a set of beliefs that guide a person or group of people. By understanding a person's ideology, it is possible to better understand why he or she acts in a certain way. In the selection below, the two speakers are discussing the traditional Islamic practice of arranging marriages. Historically, women had little or no say in whom they would marry; rather, a woman was dependent on her father or other male relatives to arrange a marriage with the person they felt was a suitable match.

Directions: Read the following passage from *Season of Migration to the North,* a work of fiction based on a real person's life and published in 1969. Then, on a separate sheet of paper, answer the questions that follow.

After a short silence he said, "Anyway if the woman's father and brothers are agreeable no one can do anything about it."

"But if she doesn't want to marry?" I said to him.

"You know how life is run here," he interrupted me. "Women belong to men, and a man's a man even if he's decrepit."

"But the world's changed," I said to him. "These are things that no longer fit in with our life in this age."

"The world hasn't changed as much as you think," said Mahjoub. "Some things have changed—pumps instead of water-wheels, iron ploughs instead of wooden ones, sending our daughters to school, radios, cars… yet even so everything's as it was." Mahjoub laughed as he said, "The world will really have changed when the likes of me become ministers in the government. And naturally that," he added, still laughing, "is an out-and-out impossibility."

1. What is the first speaker's justification for continuing arranged marriages?

_____

2. Why does the second speaker reject the first speaker's defense of arranged marriages?

_____

3. Why might a man support an ideology that treats a woman as his property? What are the drawbacks for men in supporting such an ideology?

_____

4. Why might a woman support an ideology that places her in such a role in her society? Are there any advantages she might gain by supporting such an ideology?

_____

5. At the conclusion of the passage, the first speaker suggests that the more things change, the more they stay the same. What are some ways ideology might pass from one generation to the next, thus making it appear as if little has changed?

_____

★ HISTORY AND GEOGRAPHY ACTIVITY 6

Bedouin Life

"Watering camels is hard work. They are thirsty and drink a lot, and the sun is hot. It is worse when the wind blows; then it is like a furnace. . . . Only the Bedu could endure this life," noted Wilfred Thesiger, an English explorer who crossed the Arabian Desert during the 1940s. Across the arid desert of Southwest Asia these nomads travel, searching for fresh water and pastureland for their camels, goats, and sheep. How do the bedouin survive such harsh conditions?

Searing heat and scant rainfall mean a life of hardship for the desert nomad. For thousands of years, the bedouin have moved between pasture and oasis. Members of the same clan tent together near oases during the dry season, moving their herds out to desert pastures when the winter rains come. A close-knit society

> ### Bedouin Proverb
>
> *Me and my brother against our cousin. Me, my brother, and my cousin against the stranger.*

based on tribal loyalties and alliances has ensured survival. Traditionally, the bedouin have claimed certain grazing lands as *dirah,* or tribal territory. Tribe members have continually fought to protect their lands and herds from raiding parties of other tribes. Marriage perpetuated divisions, as no member of a noble tribe would marry someone from a tribe of lesser status.

The bonds of tradition and loyalty that once made survival in the desert possible

Modernization and new sources of wealth have brought changes to bedouin Arab life. Their Islamic culture, however, remains centered on hospitality, tribal courtesy, and family relationships.

HISTORY AND GEOGRAPHY ACTIVITY 6 (continued)

have been affected by recent changes in Arab society. The vast desert that was once crossed only by camels now bears a network of roads. The bedouin use trucks to travel from place to place, taking their families, their belongings, and their animals with them. Instead of herding animals from grazing spots to water holes, they now haul water to the animals by truck. The bedouin maintain their fierce independence, however, and continue their nomadic life.

People adapt to their physical environment in different ways. The areas in which they settle, the crops they grow, how they use resources, and how they respond culturally to their surroundings reflect this process of adaptation. The bedouin developed a migratory life to find water and pastureland for their animals. They established a pattern of trade with oasis settlements, exchanging animal skins and meat for such goods as clothing and the fruit of the date palm. The harsh life of desert nomads on the Arabian Peninsula has affected other aspects of bedouin culture. Competition among tribes for limited resources such as wells and grazing areas results in raiding and blood feuds, further shaping bedouin values, customs, and loyalties.

APPLYING GEOGRAPHY TO HISTORY

Directions: Answer the questions below in the space provided.

1. How does physical environment affect people's lives?

   _____

   _____

2. What are some examples of adaptation to physical environment?

   _____

3. Why would family ties be so important to the bedouin?

   _____

   _____

Critical Thinking

4. **Synthesizing Information** On a separate sheet of paper, write a short paragraph describing the ways in which people in your community have adapted culturally to their surroundings.

Activity

5. Research how the lives of the bedouin have changed since World War II and write a short report. In your report, address the following question: Since World War II, how have Arab governments sought to integrate the bedouin into modern Arab society? Have these methods met with success? Why or why not?

Mapping History Activity 6

Distant Outposts

During the period of Islamic civilization described in Chapter 6, the Islamic Empire had three different capitals. Madinah was the capital under the Rightly-Guided Caliphs (true followers of Muhammad). The capital of the Umayyad Empire was Damascus. The Abbasids built the city of Baghdad for their capital.

Directions: The map below shows the Islamic Empire during three different periods. Use the map to answer the questions and complete the activity that follow.

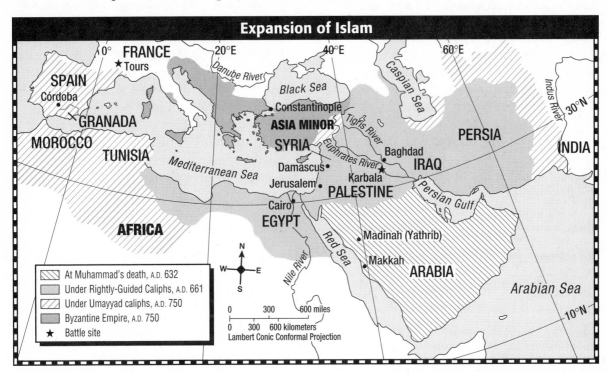

Expansion of Islam

Legend:
- At Muhammad's death, A.D. 632
- Under Rightly-Guided Caliphs, A.D. 661
- Under Umayyad caliphs, A.D. 750
- Byzantine Empire, A.D. 750
- ★ Battle site

0 300 600 miles
0 300 600 kilometers
Lambert Conic Conformal Projection

1. What is the approximate distance from Makkah to Madinah?

   _____

2. How far is Madinah from Damascus?

   _____

3. What was the primary direction of Islamic expansion from the Arabian Peninsula?

   _____

4. In what direction would pilgrims traveling from Cairo to Makkah travel?

   _____

5. The Muslim armies engaged in the jihad traveled along the North African coast to Morocco, then Spain, and north into France where their advance was stopped at the Battle of Tours. Draw the likely path followed by the armies.

6. What was the approximate distance traveled by Islamic armies from Makkah to Tours?

   _____

   _____

Historical Significance Activity 6

Islamic Architecture

One important Islamic contribution to world architecture is the mosque—the temple in which Muslims gather to worship. Although mosques, with their elaborate interior mosaics and other decorations, are often very beautiful, their purpose is to welcome and shelter the faithful. The architecture that all mosques share reflects this purpose.

The First House of Worship

Muhammad made his flight to the city of Madinah in A.D. 622. In Madinah, a community of believers gathered to worship in Muhammad's house. The design of the house was fairly simple: there was an enclosed, oval-shaped courtyard with small huts or shelters along one wall, and a covered corridor for the poor followers. Since the time of Muhammad, almost all mosques have repeated the basic shape of this first house of worship. Most mosques have an enclosed courtyard, a building at one end for reciting prayers, and two corridors on each side.

The Mosque Today

During Muhammad's first two years in Madinah, he prayed in the direction of Jerusalem. He then received a revelation that the true direction was toward Makkah, the final destination of the hajj. All mosques are designed to face toward Makkah, and a decorative recess marks that direction. Similarly, when Muhammad prayed in Madinah, he summoned people to prayer by standing on the roof. People are now called to prayer from atop a tall tower called a minaret that is either attached to the mosque or stands close to it. In many mosques, the courtyards have been expanded to accommodate increases in the number of worshipers.

Directions: Answer the following questions in the space provided.

1. What was the original design of Muhammad's house of worship in Madinah?

_____

_____

_____

2. What is the relationship between Muhammad's house in Madinah and later mosques?

_____

_____

_____

3. Use the information contained in the passage above to write a paragraph on why it might be important for Muslims to keep a strong connection between the mosque and Muhammad's original house. What might the building in which a person prays communicate about his or her religion?

_____

_____

_____

★ Cooperative Learning Activity **6** ★  ★

The Travels of Ibn Battuta

BACKGROUND

In 1325, Abu Abdullah Ibn Battuta left Tangier, Morocco, intending to perform the hajj, the once-in-a-lifetime (at least) pilgrimage to Makkah required of all Muslims. He returned 29 years later, the greatest traveler of the medieval world, having journeyed all the way to China. His travel stories from India, China, Ceylon, and other lands are filled with commentaries on Muslim beliefs and practices. Ibn Battuta's own *Rihla* (travel diaries) describe an extraordinary man and a cultural history of Islam in the medieval age. By researching Ibn Battuta's travels, you will learn more about Islamic civilization during the fourteenth century.

GROUP DIRECTIONS

1. As a group, research the travels of Ibn Battuta.

2. Brainstorm the tasks that will be required to complete the project. Create a work plan and assign specific responsibilities and schedules to individual group members.

3. The product of the research will be both a written report that may include properly footnoted quotes from Ibn Battuta's own accounts, as well as an oral presentation to the class in which all group members participate. Decide on the form of the report and presentation and identify the presentation aids, such as maps and other visuals, that will be required.

4. Appoint a group leader who will be required to prepare a separate report of reactions and observations on (a) the group's activities and (b) his or her own facilitation challenges and assessment of the group's performance.

ORGANIZING THE GROUP

1. **Decision Making/Group Work** As a group, appoint a group leader who will oversee the preparation of the written report and the oral presentation. Have the leader work with group members to determine the tasks and approaches needed to conduct the research. Determine how and in what forms the written report and oral presentation will be prepared and presented.

2. **Individual Work** Conduct research to find out as much as possible about Ibn Battuta's travels and commentaries. Trace his travels on maps and consider how to convey the information in the report and presentation. Think about how the information might be organized into a group summary presentation.

3. **Group Work/Decision Making** Share your research with your group. Invite comments on and extensions of individuals' findings and ideas. Together, decide what information to prioritize, what information is most significant, and what information will make the final report and presentation most interesting to the audience. Assign roles and tasks for preparing the report and presentation—writers, editors, illustrators, slide or overhead preparers, map makers, and so on.

Cooperative Learning Activity 6 (continued)

4. **Additional Group Work** Collaborate on the oral presentation, assigning sections to each member. Create an evaluation form to collect feedback from the class.

5. **Group Sharing** Present the findings to the class. Have the class complete the evaluation form to learn what aspects of the presentation worked well, and which aspects could be improved.

6. **Group Work** Review the evaluation forms and discuss as a group the things that worked well and the areas that needed improvement.

7. **Individual Work** The leader of the group should present his or her summary assessment of the group's efforts and of her or his own performance as leader. The leader should provide four or five "tips" on facilitating group research activities that other leaders can use in future.

CHAPTER 6

GROUP PROCESS QUESTIONS

- What is the most important thing you learned about Ibn Battuta from this activity?
- What is the most important thing you learned about Islam and Islamic history from this activity?
- What problems did you have as an individual within the group?
- How did you solve the problems?
- What one suggestion would you have for you group leader to make future group work even more effective?

Quick **CHECK** ✔

1. Was the goal of the assignment clear at all times?

   _____

   _____

2. Were you satisfied with your work on this project? Why or why not?

   _____

   _____

3. Using what you have learned, how would you advise another group that was starting the activity?

   _____

   _____

   _____

Understanding Islam

This activity is designed to provide students with the opportunity to work together to understand various aspects of Islamic history.

TEACHER MATERIAL

Learning Objective To reinforce students' understanding of people, places, events, and causes and effects related to Islam.

Activity Students will form six groups to prepare and answer questions in the categories stated above. Two teams at a time will compete in answering each other's questions. The two highest-scoring teams then compete to determine the final winner.

Teacher Preparation Collect timing devices such as stop watches. Provide enough index cards for the entire class. Make enough copies of the handout for one or two members per team.

Activity Guidelines

1. Introduce the activity. Explain that each team member will review the chapter and prepare one question and answer on one side of an index card for each of four categories: People, Places, Events, and Causes and Effects. (You may want to give an example of the last category: How did the geography of the Arabian Peninsula affect the Bedouin who lived there?) Have each team write two extra questions to avoid possible duplications.

2. Organize the class into six teams and have each team choose a captain. Students write their questions and answers, which are then assigned point values of 5, 10, 15, 20, or 25 to indicate the level of difficulty. The point value is written on each card. The team members submit their questions for review to their captain, who then separates the cards by category and replaces any duplications.

3. Assign two members of each team to serve as scorekeeper and timekeeper. Then designate three sets of two teams to compete.

4. Teams take turns asking and answering questions. Each member of the "answer" team selects a category and the point value of the question to be answered, such as People for 5 points. The opposing team captain then asks the appropriate question from the index cards. Allow 15 seconds for the answer. The team that begins continues as long as it answers correctly. Then teams switch roles.

5. The scorekeeper checks the appropriate column on the scorecard for both category and point value.

6. The team that has the highest total after 25 minutes wins. The two highest-scoring teams then meet to determine the final winner of the competition.

Understanding Islam—Scorecard

Scorecard				
Point Value	People	Places	Events	Causes and Effects
5				
10				
15				
20				
25				

Subtotals: _____ _____ _____ _____

Total: _____

Name _____ Date _____ Class _____

Time Line Activity 6

The World of Islam

DIRECTIONS: The first centuries of Islamic civilization were a time of expansion and accomplishment. Read the time line below, then answer the questions that follow.

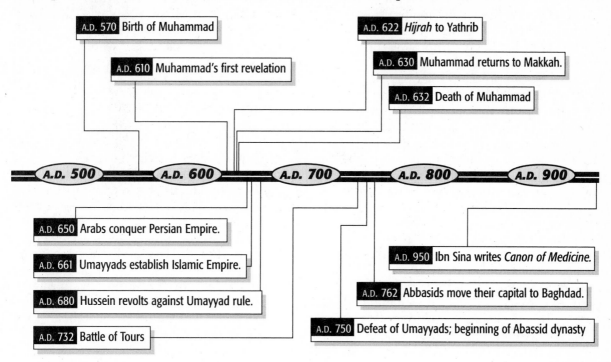

1. In A.D. 762, _____ became the new capital for the _____ dynasty.

2. Muhammad returned to Makkah in _____.

3. The Battle or Tours took place in _____.

   The _____ dynasty ruled at that time.

4. What event took place exactly a century before the Battle of Tours?

   _____

5. The *Hijrah* took place in _____.

6. The Umayyad dynasty ended in _____.

7. Muhammad experienced his first revelation in _____.

8. *Canon of Medicine* was written by _____ in

   _____.

9. The Persian Empire was conquered in _____.

10. Hussein revolted against Umayyad rule in _____.

Linking Past and Present Activity 6

Muslim Governments: Past and Present

THEN By 750, the Muslim Empire included all of Southwest Asia, Asia to the borders of India and China, most of Spain, and all of North Africa. The Muslim government was a theocracy—that is, the caliphs were religious as well as political leaders. Laws were based on the Muslim holy book, the Quran. Muslim rulers adapted laws to local practices.

Since the Quran preaches tolerance of other cultures, Muslims allowed Christians, Jews, and other groups to practice their own religions. However, citizens who embraced the teachings of Islam received special privileges.

Muslim leaders brought prosperity to the lands they controlled. Their rule of several Mediterranean countries to the east increased the flow of goods between East and West. Muslim leaders made many improvements in the empire. For example, they increased agricultural yield in Persia by building advanced irrigation systems. In addition, strong Muslim governments brought order to areas formerly torn by civil strife. This enabled people—both citizens and foreigners—to travel safely throughout the empire. This helped to encourage trade among countries in the empire.

The peace and prosperity of the Muslim Empire encouraged learning. The Muslims not only protected the arts and sciences of their citizens, they adapted them to Arabic culture. It is to the Arabs that we owe our use of the Indian numerical system and the preservation of classical Greek and Roman learning.

NOW Countries of the Middle East and North Africa are still predominantly Muslim. Islamic influence is increasing in non-Muslim countries, such as those in sub-Saharan Africa.

Government in Muslim countries takes one of two forms—secular or Islamic revivalist. Over the years, the leaders of secular Muslim countries—such as Egypt and Jordan—have worked to modernize their states. Yet some of these rulers, such as Iran's Shah Muhammad Reza Pahlavi (ruled 1941–1979), were considered by many to be corrupt and dictatorial. Rebels replaced the Shah with Ayatollah Ruhollah Khomeini, a religious leader. Khomeini strictly enforced the laws of the Quran. With the death of Khomeini in 1989, Iran has slowly begun to soften its conservative religious leanings.

Most revivalist Islamic states see Western nations as an enemy. The latter have aroused Muslim resentment by supporting secular Muslim states and by continuing to support the existence of the Jewish state of Israel. One anti-Western revivalist group, the Taliban, controlled most of Afghanistan from the mid-1990s until 2001. Taliban rule was extremely repressive. The Taliban destroyed ancient Buddhist statues, banned television, made teaching about Christianity punishable by death, and suppressed the rights of women.

In secular Muslim countries, revivalists work against the existing government. Some revivalist groups engage in terrorist activities aimed at their countries' leaders, Israel, and Western nations.

CRITICAL THINKING

Directions: Answer the following questions on a separate sheet of paper.

1. **Recognizing cause and effect:** How did Muslim leaders guard against uprisings among their subject peoples?
2. **Comparing and contrasting:** How is the attitude of modern revivalist Muslims toward other cultures different from that of the rulers of the Muslim Empire?

3. **Extending prior knowledge:** Use information you already have to explain why some Muslims resent Westerners and Israelis. Do research in the library and on the Internet to enrich your explanation with historical events that may have led up to the current state of affairs in much of the Muslim world. Present your findings in a written outline.

People in World History Activity 6

Profile 1

Umar (c. 581–644)

The first four caliphs, or successors to Muhammad, are called "the Rightly Guided Caliphs." All four were close friends or relatives of Muhammad, and all worked to protect and spread the word of Islam. All of these men are revered within the Islamic tradition. The second of these caliphs, Umar ibn al-Khattab, or Umar, holds a special place. For it was Umar who led the conquests that would spread Arab culture and the Islamic faith throughout Southwest Asia and North Africa. The results of his conquests have fundamentally affected the life of the peoples of these regions ever since.

Like Muhammad, Umar was born in Makkah. Like many others, he was at first hostile to Muhammad and his teachings. By 618, however, he had converted to Islam and became one of Muhammad's close advisers. He supported Abu Bakr, Muhammad's father-in-law, as the first caliph. Abu Bakr named Umar as his successor in 634. From this time until his death 10 years later, Umar would do more to spread Islam than anyone except Muhammad himself.

Above all else, Umar was an expansionist general who led the Arabs on a series of victories. Within two years of the beginning of his caliphate, his armies invaded the Byzantine Empire. In a short time, they had captured Syria and Palestine. The important cities of Damascus and Jerusalem fell to his troops. The Arabs invaded and conquered Egypt and pushed farther across northern

Umar ibn al-Khattab, top left, detail from *Zubdat al-Tawarikh* (Cream of Chronologies), Turkish, ca. 1600

Africa. They even challenged, and defeated, forces of the Persian Empire.

At the time of Muhammad's death, the Arabs controlled the Arabian Peninsula. By the end of Umar's rule, Arab territory had more than doubled, stretching north to the Black and Caspian Seas and along much of the south shore of the Mediterranean.

Umar's rule over the regions he conquered was not completely autocratic. Conquered peoples, although forced to pay tribute, were not forced to convert to Islam and were allowed to keep many of their local customs. Umar governed in a way that minimized conflict among Muslims, Christians, and Jews. His reasonable rule, however, could not save him from a violent death. A Persian slave, dissatisfied with his rule, killed Umar while he was at worship in the city of Madinah. Before he died, Umar had appointed a committee to decide on his successor. Thus, he left a legacy of a peaceful transition as well as the more enduring one of the spread of Arab culture and Islam.

REVIEWING THE PROFILE

Directions: Answer the following questions on a separate sheet of paper.

1. To what areas did Umar extend Arab and Muslim influence?

2. How did he ensure there would be a peaceful transition of leadership after his death?

3. **Critical Thinking Drawing Conclusions.** Why do you think that Umar did not force his conquered subjects to adopt Islam?

> ## People in World History Activity **6**
> ### Profile 2

Omar Khayyam (1048–1131)

Omar Khayyam was a well-known mathematician, astronomer, and poet who lived in Persia during the Middle Ages. He did important work in the mathematical field of algebra, publishing several books on the subject. He contributed to an amazingly accurate recalculation of the solar calendar at the request of the Sultan. He is also famous for his collection of short poems, *The Rubaiyat*, which was translated from Persian in 1859 and is still extremely popular.

Ghiyath al-Din Abul Fateh Omar Ibn Ibrahim al-Nisaburi al-Khayyam was born in 1044 in Nishapur in modern-day Iran.

Khayyam worked predominantly in the field of algebra, which gets its name from the Arabic word *al-jabr.* He classified cubic equations, developed the binomial theorem, and devised an approach to solving algebraic equations using geometry.

In 1074, the Sultan invited the famous mathematician to the city of Esfahan to establish an observatory. Khayyam worked there for 18 years, on a team of astronomers developing a new, more reliable calendar.

The result, the Jalal-ud-in calendar, is accurate to within one day in 3,770 years. Khayyam calculated the length of one year to be 365.24219858156 days, which is amazing for two reasons. Carrying the result to

11 decimal places shows his concern for precision. He was also exceptionally accurate. It's now known that the length of a year shortens over time in the sixth decimal place. The length of a year around the end of the 20th century is estimated at 365.242190 days.

Khayyam also was a poet, writing short, four-line poems (quatrains). His poems were collected, translated into English, and assembled into a book published in 1859. The book remains popular today. *The Rubaiyat* contains almost 500 poems, although only about 120 can be definitely ascribed to Khayyam. Many of the poems are about the joys of love, good wine, and leisure. Some readers have interpreted his poems literally, as expressing a hedonistic earthly life. Many readers see more complex spiritual meanings in his themes.

Khayyam fell from favor after the Sultan's death and retired to Nishapur, teaching and writing on mathematics until his death.

REVIEWING THE PROFILE

Directions: Answer the following questions on a separate sheet of paper.

1. In what mathematical field did Khayyam work primarily?

2. What were some of Khayyam's major achievements?

3. Why is Khayyam's calculation of the length of a year amazing?

4. **Critical Thinking** **Drawing Inferences.** During the Middle Ages, wealthy patrons would sometimes financially support academics and artists so they could concentrate on their studies. In what ways do artists and intellectuals support themselves today?

PRIMARY SOURCE READING 6

Muhammad's Wife Remembers the Prophet

Islam was spread by an Arab merchant named Muhammad (also spelled Mohammed). Upon his death, he left behind two major achievements: a monotheistic religion that stood on an equal footing with Judaism and Christianity and a well-organized political-religious community that increased the power and influence of the Arabs. What kind of man was Muhammad that he could achieve such profound changes in Arab civilization?

Muhammad's third wife was Ayesha (or A'ishah), the young daughter of one of his strongest supporters, Abu Bakr. Even though this marriage was made for political reasons, Ayesha seems to have loved and admired Muhammad. She was only 18 years old when he died, but she later became an active leader in the political struggles over who should be caliph.

Guided Reading *In this selection, read to learn what an Arab writer has recorded in an interview with Ayesha about Muhammad as a person.*

When Ayesha was questioned about Mohammed she used to say:

He was a man just such as yourselves. He laughed often and smiled much. He would mend his clothes and cobble his shoes. He used to help me in my household duties; but what he did oftenest was to sew. If he had the choice between two matters, he would choose the easiest, so long as no sin could accrue therefrom. He never took revenge excepting where the honor of God was concerned. When angry with anyone, he would say, "What hath taken such a one that he should soil his forehead in the mud."

His humility was shown by his riding on asses, by his accepting the invitations even of slaves, and when mounted, by his taking another behind him.

He would say: "I sit at meals as a servant does and I eat like a servant. For I really am a servant."

He would sit as one that was always ready to rise. He discouraged fasting that was beyond the established duty, and works of mortification. When seated with his followers, he would remain long silent at a time. In the Mosque at [Madinah], they used to repeat pieces of poetry and tell stories regarding the incidents that occurred in the "days of ignorance" and laugh; and Mohammed, listening to them, would smile at what they said.

Mohammed hated nothing more than lying.

Whenever he knew that any of his followers had erred in this respect, he would hold himself aloof from them until he was assured of their repentance.

How He Talked

He did not speak rapidly, running the words into one another, but enunciated each syllable distinctly, so that what he said was imprinted in the memory of everyone who heard him. When at public prayers, it might be known from a distance that he was reading, by the motion of his beard. . . .

He used to stand for such a long time at his prayers that his legs would swell. When remonstrated with, he said: "What! Shall I not behave as a thankful servant [of Allah] should?"

He refused to accept presents that had been offered as alms. Neither would he allow any one in his family to use what had been brought as alms. "For," said he, "alms are the impurity of mankind (meaning that which cleanses them of impurity)." His scruples on this point were so strong that he would not even eat a date picked up on the road, lest perchance it might have been dropped from a tithe load. . . .

Mohammed had a special liking for sweetmeats and honey. A tailor once invited him to his house and placed before him barley bread, with stale suet. There was also a pumpkin in the dish. Now Mohammed greatly relished the pumpkin.

31

PRIMARY SOURCE READING 6

His servant Anas used to say as he looked at a pumpkin: "Dear little plant, how the Prophet loved thee!"

When Mohammed ate fresh dates he would keep the bad dates in his hand. Someone asked him on a certain occasion to give him the dates he had rejected. "Not so," Mohammed answered, "What I do not like myself, I do not like to give another."

Once a trayful of fresh dates was brought to him. He set it down on his knees and, taking them up by handfuls, sent a handful to each of his wives. Then, taking another handful, he ate it himself. He kept throwing the stones [pits] to his left side, and the domestic fowl came and ate them up.

. . . He never ate reclining for [the Angel] Gabriel had told him that such was the manner of kings; nor had he ever two men walk behind him. . . . When offered by Gabriel the valley of [Makkah] full of gold, he preferred to forgo it, saying that when he was hungry he would come before the Lord lowly, and when he was full, with praise.

Mohammed's Poverty at [Madinah]

Ayesha says that for months together Mohammed did not get a full meal: Months used to pass and no fire would be lighted in Mohammed's house either for baking bread or cooking meat. One night Abu Bakr sent Mohammed the leg of a kid [young goat]. I held it while the Prophet cut off a piece for himself; and in his turn the Prophet held it while I cut off a piece for myself.

"What!" exclaimed the listeners, "And ye ate without a lamp?"

"Had we possessed oil for a lamp think you not that we should have lighted it for [cooking] our food?"

INTERPRETING THE READING

Directions *Use information from the reading to answer the following questions. If necessary, use a separate sheet of paper.*

1. What actions show that Muhammad was devoutly religious?

_____

_____

2. What faults in other people made Muhammad angry?

_____

_____

Critical Thinking

3. Identifying Central Issues According to Ayesha, what kind of a man was Muhammad? Did he behave like a ruler? Explain.

_____

_____

_____

_____

_____

Reteaching Activity 6

The World of Islam

The Islamic religion greatly influenced the growth of Southwest Asia. Cultures and civilizations developed based on the teaching of the Quran. In the period between its beginnings and the Abbasid dynasty, the Islamic civilization saw many changes and developments.

DIRECTIONS: Information about the Islamic civilization is listed in the box below. Place each item under its proper heading.

• House of Wisdom	• urban civilization	• algebra
• Sunni/Shiite split	• Five Pillars of Islam	• hajj
• built powerful state	• Ibn Sina	• Harun al-Rashid
• Ibn-Rushd	• founded by Mu'awiyah	• Battle of Tours
• A.D. 661–750	• worked to ensure equality among all Muslims, Arab and non-Arab	• A.D. 750–1258
• revelations recorded in Quran		• shari'ah

Islamic Civilization

Islamic Beliefs and Practices	Umayyad Dynasty

Abbasid Dynasty	Islamic Achievements

Copyright © by The McGraw-Hill Companies, Inc.

CHAPTER 6

★ Enrichment Activity 6 ★  ★

Ramadan

As you have read, fasting is one of the Five Pillars of Islam, and the month-long fast that occurs during the month of Ramadan is required of all adult Muslims. As the following passage explains, the fast begins each day at dawn, at the moment when "white thread becomes distinct from black thread," and does not end until sunset.

> Ramazan [Ramadan] . . . is an occasion during which believers are thought to be closer to God. Ramazan is a month-long period of fasting, somewhat like Lent only more stringent. It is a time of atonement. It is the month in which the [Quran] was allegedly revealed to [Muhammad]. It is said: "When the noble time of Ramazan comes, the doors of heaven are opened, the doors of hell closed, and the devils tied down." In other words, people's souls are opened to God and closed to **şeytan** (devils); they are sustained by God as by food.
>
> During Ramazan the faithful keep a fast (**oruç**). All day, from before sunrise to after sunset, one must abstain from food and drink. . . . It is also not permissible to smoke, take medicine, or chew gum; in other words, no substance may enter the body. One must be separated from those things which promote and sustain life in its material earthly form; fasting is a way to remind people of their dependence on God for these things. **Oruç** is felt to be a great **sevap** (good work) by which God is pleased; if faithfully performed, it is believed to bring a remission of sins.
>
> —From *The Seed and the Soil: Gender and Cosmology in Turkish Village Society* by Carol Delaney, copyright © 1991 by the Regents of the University of California.

Directions: Answer the questions below in the space provided.

1. Why do the followers of Islam believe they are brought closer to God through their long period of fasting? _____

2. How are the body and the soul, and the gates of heaven and hell, thought to mirror each other during the fast? _____

_____

3. The twenty-sixth night of Ramadan is called the "Night of Determination." According to the Quran, it is on this night that God will decide the destiny of the entire world for the course of the following year. How does this night correspond to the objectives of the rest of the fast? Support your response with details from the passage. _____

_____

4. Take a moment to consider all the food you consume on an average day. How would you feel if you had to undergo a month-long fast? _____

_____

5. You may be surprised to learn that Ramadan is usually thought of by Muslims as a time of celebration. After a long day of fasting, a light meal is enjoyed by neighbors and friends. Why might Ramadan be considered a time of social solidarity and enjoyment rather than simply one of hardship? _____

World Art and Music Activity 6

Islamic Textiles

Islamic carpets and silks are works of art. They use bold colors and incorporate geometric shapes, flowers and trees, real and mythical animals, and inscriptions. How did this artistic tradition develop?

Directions: Read the passage below, then answer the questions in the space provided.

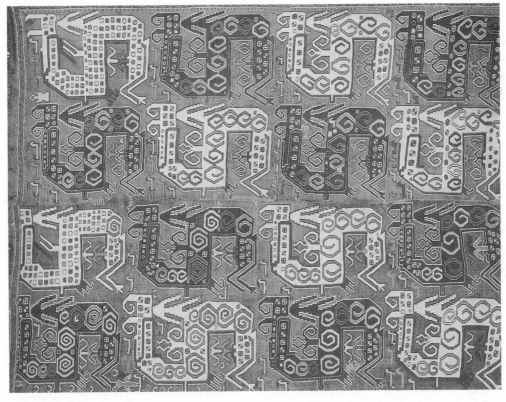

Islamic carpet (detail)

Rugs are walked on, clothing is worn out, and even fabric hanging on the wall fades and tears. Because of its dual aesthetic and practical functions, much Islamic textile work does not hold up over long periods of time. The examples that remain, however, display originality, creativity, and artistic ability within a strictly defined religious atmosphere.

The Quran teaches that art should inspire contemplation and prayer. According to Muhammad, only God can make a human figure. Therefore Islamic artists are forbidden to recreate the human form in artistic representations. The restrictions inspired past artists to create art that moved away from explicit representations of the real world and instead employed patterns and geometric shapes. These patterns illustrate a highly developed aesthetic sense that often emphasizes symmetry, repetition, and proportion. Later Islamic sects were less strict and allowed artists to incorporate real figures into their artworks as long as there was no religious connection.

(continued)

World Art and Music Activity 6

Some of the most highly valued objects in the Islamic world were carpets. Not only did these carpets serve utilitarian or religious purposes (such as prayer rugs), but they were also used as gifts, rewards, and signs of political favor. Carpet-making was highly developed in Iran, where a great, royal carpet could have more than 300 knots per square inch. Some carpets, with their intricate designs and tightly woven piles, could take a single weaver more than 20 years to complete. Many carpets were designed to look like gardens, something that was highly valued in such an arid land.

Another important Islamic art form was the illuminated manuscript. These took the form of either beautifully adorned pages from the Quran or imaginative and richly colored illustrations of romances, historical accounts, and fables. Because of religious constraints, many artists concentrated their efforts on lovingly and painstakingly copying the sacred text of the Quran to such a degree that it developed into a separate art form–what we know today as calligraphy.

Due to the nomadic lifestyles of many early Islamic peoples, much of their textile art was portable. Rugs were carried for personal use throughout the common trade routes. As rugs and other Islamic textiles began to be traded, they influenced the art of India and the Western world. The influence of Islamic art in Europe can be found in the art from both the Medieval and Renaissance periods in which the arabesque design, a commonly-found Islamic pattern of interlaced lines, was frequently used in tapestries, manuscripts, and wood carvings.

Reviewing the Selection

1. How is the carpet shown typical of Islamic textiles?

_____

_____

2. Why do most Islamic textiles show patterns instead of human figures?

_____

_____

Critical Thinking

3. Making Inferences Why do you think carpets were so highly valued?

_____

_____

_____

4. Drawing Conclusions Do you think the Islamic religious restrictions helped or hindered the development of textile art?

_____

_____

_____

_____

Glencoe

WORLD HISTORY

Chapter 6
Section Resources

SECTIONS

Guided Reading Activity 6-1

The Rise of Islam

DIRECTIONS: Answer the following questions as you read Section 1.

1. What language did the Arabs speak and where did they live?

_____

2. How were Arabian tribes ruled and how were the rulers selected?

_____

_____

3. What accomplishment made it possible for the Arabs to begin to take part in the caravan trade?

_____

4. What object became the principal object of worship among the Arabs?

_____

_____

5. As Muhammad grew to manhood, what did he find troubling within his culture?

_____

_____

6. What do Muslims believe was given to Muhammad while he meditated alone in the hills?

_____

_____

7. What written document resulted from Muhammad's revelations from Allah?

_____

8. Define the *Hijrah.*

_____

_____

9. What are three similarities between Islam, Christianity, and Judaism?

_____

_____

10. What is a difference between Islam and Christianity?

_____

11. Name the Five Pillars of Islam.

_____

_____

SECTION 6-1

Guided Reading Activity 6-2

The Arab Empire and Its Successors

DIRECTIONS: As you are reading the section, decide if a statement is true or false. Write **T** if the statement is true or **F** if the statement is false. For all false statements write a corrected statement.

_____ **1.** Muhammad left clear instructions as to who would succeed him at death.

_____

_____ **2.** Raiding one's enemies was known in the Quran as the "struggle in the way of God" or jihad.

_____

_____ **3.** The courage of the Arab soldiers was enhanced by the fact that they had superior weapons to most of their enemies.

_____

_____ **4.** The general Mu'awiyah was known for one outstanding trait: he used more force than necessary whether it was needed or not.

_____

_____ **5.** Mu'awiyah moved the capital of the Arab Empire from Madinah to Damascus, Syria.

_____

_____ **6.** Arab expansion in Europe came to a halt because of geographical barriers that stood in the way of advancing Arab armies.

_____

_____ **7.** The Shiite Muslims accept only the descendants of Ali as the true rulers of Islam, while the Sunni Muslims claim the descendants of the Umayyads were the true caliphs.

_____

_____ **8.** In 1187, Saladin's army invaded the kingdom of Jerusalem and destroyed the Christian forces there.

_____

_____ **9.** As a result of the Mongol destruction of Baghdad, the new center of Islamic civilization became Cairo, in Egypt.

_____

Guided Reading Activity 6-3

Islamic Civilization

DIRECTIONS: Fill in the blanks below as you read Section 3.

For the most part, the period of the Arab Empire was **(1)** _____.
Trade was carried both by ship and by **(2)** _____ caravans, which
traveled from Morocco in the far west to the countries beyond the Caspian Sea. The
development of **(3)** _____ and the use of **(4)** _____
made it easier to exchange goods.

(5) _____, **(6)** _____, and
(7) _____ were the centers of administrative, cultural, and economic
activity for their regions. Usually the most impressive urban buildings were the
(8) _____ for the caliphs and the great **(9)** _____ for
worship. Rules for sale of meat in the market stated, "Grilled meats should only be
made with **(10)** _____ meat and not with meat coming from a sick
animal and bought for its cheapness."

To be a Muslim is not simply to worship Allah but also to live one's life according to Allah's teachings as revealed in the **(11)** _____. According to
Islam, all peoples are equal in the eyes of Allah except one; **(12)** _____
were not considered equal. Slavery was **(13)** _____ in the Islamic
world.

The Quran granted women **(14)** _____ and
(15) _____ equality with men. Both had **(16)** _____
and **(17)** _____. Most men had only one wife because the men were
required to pay **(18)** _____ to their bride. Women had the right to
freely enter into marriage, but they also had the right of **(19)** _____.

📖 Guided Reading Activity 6-4

The Culture of Islam

DIRECTIONS: Fill in the blanks below as you read Section 4.

1. Arabs were not only aware of Greek _____, they were translating works by _____ and _____ into Arabic.

2. The Muslims adopted and passed on the _____ system of India, including the use of the zero.

3. They also perfected the _____, an instrument that made it possible for Europeans to sail to the Americas.

4. Ibn-Khaldun, who lived in the fourteenth century, was the most prominent Muslim _____ of the age.

5. One of the most familiar works of Middle Eastern literature is the _____ of Omar Khayyám.

6. The Great Mosque of _____ in present-day _____ is the largest mosque ever built, covering 10 acres.

7. Because the Muslim religion combines _____ and _____ power in one, palaces also reflected the glory of Islam.

8. One feature of these palaces that looked like castles was a _____ over the entrance gate with holes through which _____ could be poured down on the heads of attacking forces.

9. The finest example of the Islamic palace is the fourteenth-century _____ in Spain.

10. No _____ of the prophet Muhammad ever adorns a mosque, in painting or in any other art form.

SECTION 6-4

Glencoe

WORLD HISTORY

Chapter 7 Resources
Early African Civilizations, 2000 B.C.–A.D. 1500

✏️ Vocabulary Activity 7

Early African Civilizations, 2000 B.C.–A.D. 1500

DIRECTIONS: Fill in the term for each definition listed below, writing one letter in each square. Then use the letters in the shaded squares to answer the question that follows.

1. a society populated by a variety of different ethnic groups
2. a society that traces its descent through the mother
3. treeless grasslands
4. a mixed African-Arabian culture found throughout East Africa
5. a high, flat area of land
6. people who predict events by supernatural means
7. alloy used to create statues and sculptures in Ife and Benin

8. a company of travelers using camels to cross the Sahara
9. a legend or story passed down from generation to generation by word of mouth (two words)
10. storytellers who pass on a community's history, legends, and traditions
11. building used as a Muslim house of worship
12. first great African trading state

13. What do you call the type of culture and society developed by a particular region or nation?

_____

Skills Reinforcement Activity 7

Using a Computerized Card Catalog

A computerized card catalog can help you find a specific book or a variety of resources about a research topic. Usually, you begin by requesting a particular kind of search, such as a title search, a search by author's name, or a search of materials on a general subject. Once you have located an item you want, you can check its call number, availability, or other information—such as date of publication.

DIRECTIONS: Study the results of a computerized card catalog search below. Then answer the following questions in the space provided.

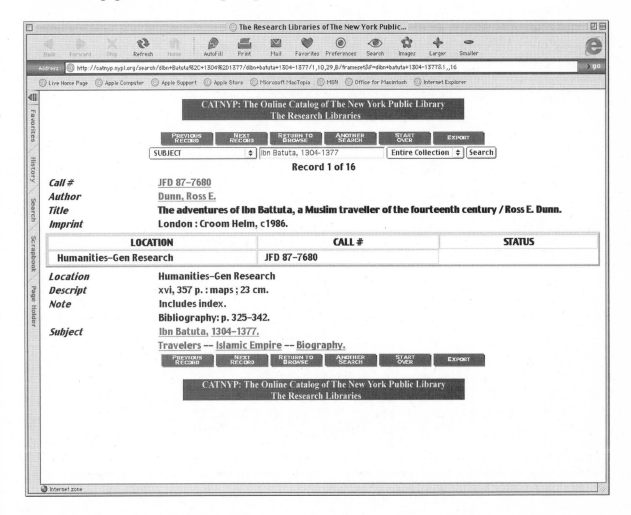

1. What is the subject of the search? _____

2. Where in the library would you find this book? _____

3. When and where was this book published? _____

4. How long is the book? _____

Critical Thinking Skills Activity 7 | Distinguishing Fact From Opinion

A fact is a statement that can be proved. An opinion is a personal belief. To distinguish between fact and opinion, look for statements that you can check for accuracy. Facts can be verified, or matched to those in other sources. Statements containing words or phrases such as *should, must, always,* *never, all, none, the most important,* or *the most interesting* are often opinions. Opinions cannot be proved. For example, it is a fact that Mount Kilimanjaro is the tallest mountain in Africa. The statement that Victoria Falls in Africa is the most beautiful waterfall in the world is an opinion.

DIRECTIONS: Read the following newspaper headlines. Mark each with an **F** if it states a fact or an **O** if it expresses an opinion.

1. _____ Early African Cultures Developed Technologies

2. _____ Early African Cultures Used Resources Wisely

3. _____ Nubian People Were Ruthless Warriors

4. _____ Nubian People Mastered the Bow and Arrow

5. _____ Matrilineal Societies Common Among Villages

6. _____ Bride's Worth Needs to be Lowered

7. _____ African Marriage Customs Outmoded

8. _____ African Communities Rely on Family Loyalties

DIRECTIONS: Read the following newspaper articles. Write a possible headline for each article based on the information given and state whether your headline expresses a fact or an opinion.

9. _____   10. _____

Music rich in rhythm was interwoven with the fabric of everyday African life. It included choral singing, music performed at royal courts, and songs and dances for ceremonies. In villages, where many activities were performed by groups, music often provided the motivation and rhythm for various tasks, such as digging ditches or pounding grain. African musicians used a variety of drums as well as harps, flutes, pipes, horns, and xylophones.

The kingdom of Ghana became one of the richest trading civilizations in Africa due to its location midway between Saharan salt mines and tropical gold mines. Between A.D. 300 and A.D. 1200 the kings of Ghana controlled a trading empire that stretched more than 100,000 square miles (260,000 square kilometers). They prospered from the taxes they imposed on goods that entered or left their kingdom. Because the ghana, or king, ruled such a vast region, the land became known by the name of its ruler—Ghana.

★ HISTORY AND GEOGRAPHY ACTIVITY 7

The Discovery of Jenne-jeno

Artifacts from the first archaeological dig at Jenne-jeno raised many questions. When archaeologists Susan and Roderick McIntosh returned to Mali in 1981, they hoped to unearth more remains that would prove Jenne-jeno was the oldest city in West Africa. Why do you think that this once thriving city was abandoned in about A.D. 1400?

After a month of labor in the hot sun and fierce winds of the Niger River, the McIntoshes' 1981 excavation unlocked some of the mysteries of how Jenne-jeno had changed over hundreds of years. The oldest artifacts indicated that the people living there around 275 B.C. fished, herded animals, and lived in circular houses.

But the most remarkable finds were the remains of workshops for making copper and iron utensils, since the nearest deposits

Finding West Africa's Oldest City

Our luck far exceeded expectations. Each of the four pits we dug yielded abundant evidence. . . . Animal bones, rice chaff, and carbonized grains documented a mixed diet. Pottery fragments, spindle whorls, terra-cotta statuary, and crucibles for smelting copper or gold gave insight into local arts and crafts. Walls defined sturdy homes.

—Susan and Roderick McIntosh, in an account of their 1981 dig

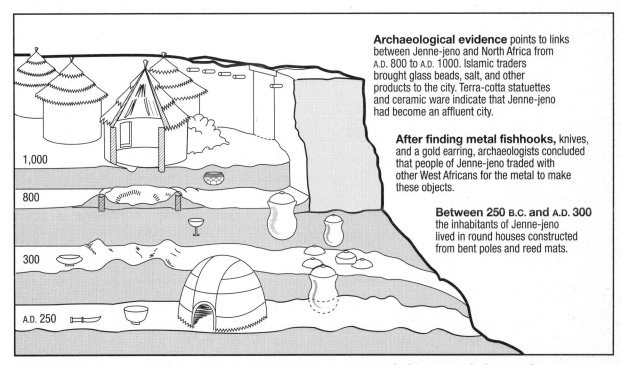

Archaeological evidence points to links between Jenne-jeno and North Africa from A.D. 800 to A.D. 1000. Islamic traders brought glass beads, salt, and other products to the city. Terra-cotta statuettes and ceramic ware indicate that Jenne-jeno had become an affluent city.

After finding metal fishhooks, knives, and a gold earring, archaeologists concluded that people of Jenne-jeno traded with other West Africans for the metal to make these objects.

Between 250 B.C. and A.D. 300 the inhabitants of Jenne-jeno lived in round houses constructed from bent poles and reed mats.

1,000

800

300

A.D. 250

A pattern of trade emerged from artifacts found at Jenne-jeno. Inhabitants traded crops they grew on the surrounding floodplain for metal to make knives, spears, and fishhooks.

HISTORY AND GEOGRAPHY ACTIVITY 7 (continued)

of iron ore and copper were 31 miles (50 km) away. The metal artifacts dated 400 years before the arrival of Islamic traders in West Africa.

People develop land for many uses—for houses, factories, public buildings, and recreation. Patterns of land use emerge and then change as development continues. Whether land is used for highways, industrial parks, or conservation areas, its use reflects the needs and values of the inhabitants of a place.

By looking at the artifacts that people left many years ago, the McIntoshes were able to reconstruct a picture of the physical characteristics of Jenne-jeno and its cultural life. They studied the customs of people living in the modern city of Jenne and found links to the social and commercial life of the people of Jenne-jeno.

APPLYING GEOGRAPHY TO HISTORY

DIRECTIONS: Answer the questions below in the space provided.

1. How do human actions affect the character of a place over time?

2. Which artifacts indicate that people in Jenne-jeno lived near a river?

3. In what way do you think trade might have led to continuing changes in Jenne-jeno?

Critical Thinking

4. **Demonstrating Reasoned Judgment** The McIntoshes found evidence of a city wall built about A.D. 1000. How would this evidence indicate that Jenne-jeno was changing?

5. **Analyzing Information** Archaeologists piece together a story about a place from the artifacts they find. How do you think the terra-cotta statuettes fit into the cultural life of the people of Jenne-jeno?

Activity

6. Research how land use has changed in your community. Use maps to show the changes that have occurred. Write a brief report explaining how these changes are linked to changes in human activities in your community or region.

Mapping History Activity 7

Trade Across North Africa

Around the year A.D. 1000, African civilizations flourished. As their wealth increased, they began to establish trade routes to exchange their products for goods that they were unable to produce themselves. In particular, the kingdoms of West Africa grew rich because of trading. The most important city in this continental trade was Timbuktu, which then became a center for learning and Islamic scholarship.

DIRECTIONS: Use the map below to answer the questions and complete the activity that follow.

1. Timbuktu was a city found in which kingdoms?

   _____

   _____

2. Which waterway was most important for the people of Timbuktu?

   _____

3. Name the important port cities of North Africa.

   _____

   _____

   _____

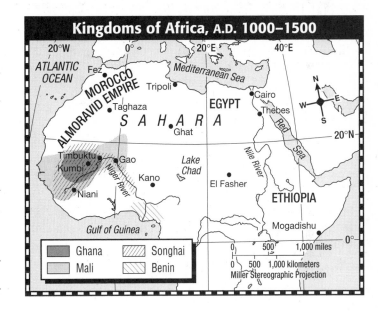

4. Read the following historical description of North African trading. Using the information provided in the paragraph, add arrows to the map above to indicate trade routes.

Salt was so common in the village of Taghaza that houses were built out of it. The people of Timbuktu needed salt to preserve and flavor food. It was also necessary for good health, since in hot climates, the human body loses salt through perspiration. The people of North Africa wanted gold, which was very plentiful in the area called Waranga located south of Niani. Timbuktu grew rich because it was about halfway between Waranga and Taghaza. Merchants came to Timbuktu to exchange salt for gold.

Other trade routes opened up as well. European goods were imported into Africa via Fez, where merchants from Timbuktu and Taghaza traded gold for them. Other traders traveled down the Niger River and then to Kano and El Fasher, before traveling down the Nile to buy Asian goods arriving at the port of Cairo. Asian goods coming from the Middle East were also shipped along the Mediterranean coast to Tripoli, where merchants coming from Timbuktu via Ghat came to trade.

49

Historical Significance Activity 7

Importing and Exporting

The kingdoms of Africa grew wealthy through trade, especially through trading gold in the kingdoms of Ghana, Mali, and Songhai. Trade was vital for these kingdoms to obtain what they did not have themselves. It resulted in links with the rest of the world as far away as China. Today, African nations still carry out much trade.

Africa is an important source of natural resources such as gold, diamonds, oil, uranium, cocoa, coffee, and lumber. Look at the charts below showing the imports and exports of three modern African nations that exist near to where ancient African civilizations existed.

GHANA

Chief exports: cocoa, wood, gold, diamonds, manganese

Exports mainly go to: United Kingdom, United States, Germany, France

Chief imports: textiles, manufactured goods, foodstuffs, fuels

Imports mainly come from: United Kingdom, United States, other European Union countries

MALI

Chief exports: livestock, peanuts, dried fish, cotton, animal skins

Exports mainly go to: European Union, western Africa

Chief imports: textiles, vehicles, petroleum products, machinery

Imports mainly come from: European Union countries

TANZANIA

Chief exports: coffee, cotton, sisal, cashew nuts, meat, cloves

Exports mainly go to: Germany, United Kingdom, United States

Chief imports: manufactured goods, machinery, transport equipment, textiles, crude oil, foodstuffs

Imports mainly come from: Germany, United Kingdom, United States, Iran (formerly Persia)

DIRECTIONS: Answer the following questions on a separate sheet of paper.

1. Who were the early African kingdoms' major trading partners?

2. Who are the major trading partners of modern African nations?

3. Take a look at the products exported. Would you characterize them as natural and agricultural products or finished products and manufactured goods?

4. How would you characterize the imports?

5. Write a short essay comparing Africa's ancient trade patterns with those of today. Are the products the same? The trading partners? Explain why they are or are not different.

★ Cooperative Learning Activity 7 ★

The Geography of Africa

BACKGROUND
The African continent is made up of several geographically and climatically different regions, all of which have been homelands to unique cultures and civilizations.
The African continent is vast, second in size only to Asia. This cooperative learning
activity uses group research and map-making skills to improve your understanding
of African geography and climates.

GROUP DIRECTIONS

1. Research Chapter 7 of your textbook and other reference sources such as geography books and atlases to gain an overview of Africa's geographic zones. Then
   assign specific geographic zones to pairs of students or individuals to research
   more thoroughly. As a group, agree upon what information about each zone is
   needed.

2. Have the "zone experts" prepare maps of the region assigned to them. Maps
   must show major geographic features, such as landmarks, bodies of water, vegetation patterns, and so on. Maps should also indicate any civilizations up to
   and including A.D. 1500 with appropriate dates.

3. The maps should be presented to and shared with the group. The various
   regional maps should be combined into a map of the entire continent. The complete Africa map will be shared with the class as a whole.

4. As a group, discuss how geography influenced and shaped any cultures or civilizations that emerged in Africa.

5. Post the maps where they can be used as reference by the class or make copies
   for distribution to the class.

ORGANIZING THE GROUP

1. **Decision Making** As a group, create a map of Africa and assign to individuals
   the various major geographic zones that should be researched and mapped.
   Provide copies of the map for each group member to use in their research.
   Reach an agreement on what physical, climatic, and other features should be
   listed in the map-based summaries of the geographic zones.

2. **Individual Work** Do research to find out as much as possible about the African
   geographic zone assigned to you. Think about what geographic factors would
   most directly influence human civilization in that area. Prepare a map of your
   zone showing whatever characteristics your group determined are needed. If
   you find useful information about one of the other geographic zones, share that
   information or the source with the group member assigned to that zone.

Cooperative Learning Activity 7 (continued)

3. **Group Work/Decision Making** Share your research in map form with your group. Invite comments on inclusions and possible omissions of data and on the effectiveness of the map's visual impact. Together, decide what information to prioritize—which information is most essential for helping the class to understand the diversity and complexity of African geography.

4. **Group Work** Combine the individual maps into the group map, using consistent colors, shading, and symbols. Create a map key to help others understand the map.

5. **Group Sharing** Present the group's map to the class, along with a brief summary of how geography affected the development of human civilizations on the continent.

GROUP PROCESS QUESTIONS

- What is the most important thing you learned about summarizing and conveying information using maps from this activity?
- What part of the project did you enjoy most?
- Were maps the best way to convey and share the information about geographic zones?

Quick CHECK ✔

1. Was the goal of the assignment clear at all times?

_____

_____

2. How was map-making different from other types of presentation techniques?

_____

_____

3. Did you have problems working together? If so, how did you solve them?

_____

_____

4. Were you satisfied with your work on this project? Why or why not?

_____

_____

_____

HISTORY SIMULATION ACTIVITY 7

Culture Quest

The ancient African kingdoms of Kush, Axum, Mali, and the East African city-states grew and developed in concert with other cultures. Each civilization borrowed or modified a cultural element from a neighboring group of people, from those they traded with, or through conquest or travel. When a group of people borrows the language, religion, or customs of another culture, that group of people exhibits evidence of cultural diffusion.

TEACHER MATERIAL

Learning Objective To identify evidence of cultural diffusion among the early African kingdoms and within the students' own community.

Activity In groups of five or six, students will find evidence from their textbooks or library resources of cultural diffusion in the ancient African kingdoms of Kush, Axum, Mali, and the East African city-states. Students will brainstorm evidence of cultural diffusion in their own community.

Teacher Preparation Bring to class the following items or close substitutes:

- reference books with illustrations demonstrating some of the cultural influences on the household objects, architecture, foods, or clothing of the early African civilizations. Examples: Kush—Roman, Assyrian, Egyptian influences; Axum—Egyptian, Greek, Roman, Persian, Indian influences; Mali—Arab world, Persian, Spanish influences; East Africa—Arab world, Indian, Persian, Chinese, Portuguese influences

- drawing paper

- 1 copy of the chart on the next page for each group

Activity Guidelines

1. Organize the class into small groups. Explain that they will find evidence from their textbooks and library resources of cultural diffusion occurring in early African kingdoms. They should also brainstorm ideas about

how their own community reflects cultural diffusion. Explain that groups will be evaluated on organization, cooperation, and factual accuracy.

2. Have each group select a manager, an artist, and a recorder.

3. Give each group recorder a copy of the chart on the next page.

4. Instruct students to work together to find each cultural group in the textbook and identify all the outside influences that affected that culture. Remind students of the means of cultural diffusion—contact with other peoples through migrations, trade, invasions, or geographical necessities. Then have students brainstorm ideas about how their own community demonstrates cultural diffusion from several cultures.

5. The recorder writes the information on the chart and cites the references.

6. The artist draws a sketch to represent the cultural element that was adopted by the civilization. Example: Kush—Egyptian pyramids.

7. Bring all the groups together to compare their answers. Have them evaluate themselves on cooperation, organization, and factual accuracy. Then discuss the cultural elements they found that exist in their own community.

HANDOUT MATERIAL

Culture Quest—Evidence Chart

Use your textbook and library resources to find evidence of cultural diffusion among the early African kingdoms listed on the chart. Then list some of the ways in which your community reflects cultural diffusion.

CULTURAL DIFFUSION CHART

Civilization	Outside Influences	Text Pages
Kush		
Axum		
Mali		
East Africa		
Your Community		

Time Line Activity 7

Early African Civilizations

DIRECTIONS: Much of Africa's history was driven by the availability of resources and trade. Contact between civilizations often resulted in the conquest of one over another. Read the time line below, then answer the questions that follow.

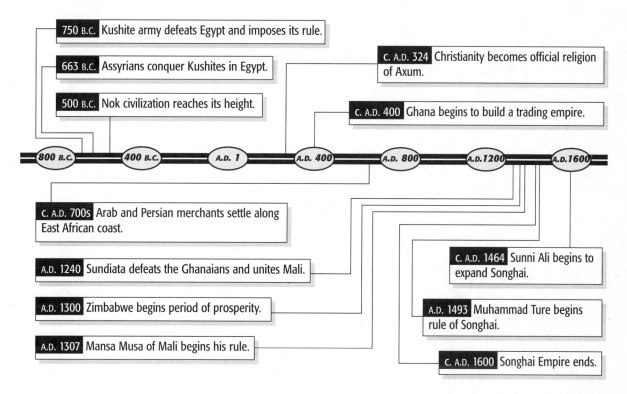

1. The kingdom of Mali eventually conquered the kingdom of Ghana's territory. About how long did the kingdom of Ghana last? _____

2. When did merchants from the Arabian Peninsula begin to settle in East Africa?

   _____

3. How long did Kushite rule over Egypt last? _____

4. When did Mansa Musa become Mali's king? _____

5. What change took place in Axum during the fourth century A.D.?

   _____

6. Approximately how long did the Songhai Empire last? _____

7. How many years were between the beginning of Ghana's trading empire and Zimbabwe's? _____

8. When did the Nok civilization reach its peak? _____

55

Linking Past and Present Activity 7

Ghana: Ancient Empire, Modern Nation

THEN The Soninke, a group of people who lived northeast of the Senegal River, founded Ghana. Because of their agricultural skill and efficient system of irrigation, the Soninke were able to raise enough food to support a population of 200,000 people.

Ghana means "war chief" and reflects the Soninke's pride in being warriors. By 300, the Soninke had learned to make iron. The iron weapons they forged gave the Soninke an advantage over neighboring groups, whose weapons were made from ebony wood.

In 992, the Soninke took over a Berber town near an important caravan route. Soninke command of this route financed their military expansion. By 1000, the Ghanaian Empire had grown to be about the size of Texas.

Ghana developed into a trade center that attracted caravans of Muslim merchants. The many mines in Ghana and its subject countries were the source of the empire's most famous export—gold. The people of Ghana also traded slaves, ivory, tools, and weapons for the copper, salt, and cloth brought by the Muslims.

Ghanaian kings were considered to be sacred. A council of ministers advised the king and carried out his decisions. Over time, an ever-increasing number of Muslims began to move into Ghana. Their influence on Ghanaian affairs began to grow. Many became ministers, helping to set Ghana's political and economic policies. Their presence, however, had little effect on religion.

NOW Present-day Ghana is located a good distance south of the long-gone Ghanaian Empire. Nonetheless, the inhabitants of modern-day Ghana consider the glory of old Ghana to be part of their cultural heritage. Ghanaians are also proud of the fact that Ghana was the first black African colony to become fully self-governing.

In 1981, following a series of corrupt and incompetent leaders, Jerry Rawlings took charge of Ghana, turning around its tottering economy and initiating many important reforms. By 1986 Ghana had become known as "Black Africa's Economic Showcase." In 1991, Ghana changed from a one-party to a multiparty government. In 1992, a new constitution gave political parties the freedom to organize. President Rawlings still headed Ghana's government in 2001.

Like the old empire, the new Ghana exports large amounts of gold. Its excellent cocoa is also important to the economy. Modernization has helped Ghanaian businesses. One of Rawlings's great achievements was to expand the nation's access to electricity. In 1981 only 12 percent of the population had electricity. In 2001 this increased to 50 percent of the nation. While under British control, many Ghanaians became Christians. Today the population includes about twice as many Christians as Muslims. About 35 percent of the people practice ancestral religions.

Ghanaians express national pride through their craftwork. Their kente cloth and carved goods are known all over the world.

CRITICAL THINKING

Directions: Answer the following questions on a separate sheet of paper.

1. **Drawing conclusions:** What does the name *Ghana* tell us about the people who founded the empire?
2. **Comparing and contrasting:** What do the economies of ancient Ghana and modern Ghana have in common?

3. **Synthesizing information:** Explain why modern Ghanaians are proud of their country. Do research in the library and on the Internet to learn more about some of the ways in which Ghana has developed and prospered in the last twenty years. Write a brief report of your findings.

People in World History Activity 7

Profile 1

King Ezana (C. A.D. fourth century)

The tallest of the stelae still remaining from the Axumite civilization

The country of Ethiopia is one of the longest continually inhabited places on the earth—some of the oldest human remains ever were found there. Ethiopia has another distinction, also related to its longevity. Today, Ethiopia is considered to be one of the oldest Christian countries in the world. The man who brought Christianity to the region was King Ezana of Axum.

Axum was a great civilization that was flourishing in what is now Ethiopia by A.D. 200. Over the ages, the Axum civilization developed its own architecture, its own language, and its own written language. These writings have helped historians learn much about the events of 1,800 years ago. The written records and archaeological evidence tell the story of how Axum grew rich through trade with Egypt, Greece, Rome, India, and Persia. Even the ruins that remain of Axum's towns, trading posts, paved streets, palaces, and monuments are stunning. Among the most impressive are the stelae, or obelisks, the people of Axum built in honor of their gods. Intricately carved from single pieces of stone, many of these huge monuments are still standing. The gods of traditional Axumite religion, however, were replaced by the single Christian God at the direction of King Ezana.

The greatest leader of Axum, Ezana led the kingdom at its height in the fourth century. Axum's wealth and power came from its role as a trading powerhouse. The ships that brought goods to its port also carried people, of course—and their ideas. The people of Axum naturally absorbed some of these ideas from other cultures, all the while developing a distinct culture. One of the ideas that was absorbed was Christianity. Two Christian children who were shipwrecked off the coast were brought to the court of Ezana's father and predecessor, Ella Amida. They lived there for years, and over time, they convinced the king to convert to Christianity. After he ascended to the throne, Ezana declared Christianity the religion of Axum in A.D. 324. Significantly, coins minted during his reign include symbols of both the traditional Axumite religion and Christianity.

Ezana's decision had a huge impact on his people. The diverse, cosmopolitan nation came together under a new religion. Thus, Axum had new strength and unity and remained a force until its decline 200 years later. Nevertheless, the Christian tradition begun by King Ezana remains strong in the region.

REVIEWING THE PROFILE

Directions: Answer the following questions on a separate sheet of paper.

1. How did King Ezana learn about Christianity?

2. **Critical Thinking** Drawing Conclusions. The profile reports that coins minted during King Ezana's reign include both traditional Axumite religion and Christian symbols. What conclusion can you draw about this combination of symbols?

People in World History Activity **7**   **Profile 2**

Mansa Musa (died A.D. 1337)

Neither the man who travels nor he who stays at home has anything to fear from robbers or men of violence.

A traveler, commenting on life in Mali during Mansa Musa's time

No one knows for certain when Mansa Musa was born. He came to the throne in 1312 and ruled Mali for nearly 25 years. In time, his reign would be remembered as a golden age in the history of the region. It was certainly a peaceful time, as Musa was adept at combining strong central laws with flexibility that allowed them to conform to local practices. The quotation above is testament to the order that prevailed during Musa's reign. That same traveler also wrote that the people of Mali had "a greater abhorrence of injustice than any other people." This, perhaps, is a comment on the results of Musa's rule as well as on the character of the people themselves.

Under Musa's rule, the peace in the empire was matched by its prosperity, which was heightened by Musa's work to expand trade. Musa was also a political and military success. Mali was a huge empire that stretched from the Atlantic to deep into the African continent, and from the rain forest in the south to the Sahara in the north. In addition, historical records indicate that

Mansa Musa, King of Mali, detail from a Spanish map of West Africa, 1375

Musa was an active leader who examined and decided important legal cases himself.

Mansa Musa is perhaps best known, however, for the important role Islamic culture played in his government. A Muslim, he commissioned great mosques to be built in Timbuktu, Mali's capital, and other cities. Under Musa's patronage, Muslim scholarship flourished, and Timbuktu began its tenure as an important center of learning. Musa's pilgrimage to Makkah in 1324–1325 is recorded as a grand procession of more than 12,000 enslaved persons carrying gold. This public display of wealth and power enhanced Mali's reputation and prestige throughout the world.

REVIEWING THE PROFILE

Directions: Answer the following questions on a separate sheet of paper.

1. What are some of Mansa Musa's accomplishments?

2. Why was his reign remembered as a "golden age"?

3. How did Mansa Musa apply law to help bring about peaceful times?

4. What religion influenced Mansa Musa's government?

5. **Critical Thinking** Formulating Questions. Write five questions you have about Mansa Musa and his reign. Then conduct research to find the answers.

PRIMARY SOURCE READING 7

A Visit to Zeila and Mogadishu

The Muslim writer Ibn Battuta was one of the greatest travelers of the Middle Ages. During the 1300s, he traveled through Africa and east-ward to India and China. Traveling by small ship or by caravan through deserts and wild mountain country, he met many of the most famous kings and conquerors of his time. In the excerpt that follows, Ibn Battuta describes a visit to East Africa in 1331.

Guided Reading *In this selection, read to learn how Zeila and Mogadishu developed into two different and yet similar towns.*

. . . I travelled by sea for four days and arrived at the town of Zeila. It is the capital of Berbera: the inhabitants are black, and follow Shafi'i [Islamic] rite. The country is a desert which stretches for two months' march, starting at Zeila and finishing at Mogadishu. Their beasts of burden are camels, and they also possess sheep which are famous for their butter. The people are dark-skinned and very many of them are heretics.

Zeila is a large town with an important mar-ket; but it is one of the dirtiest towns in exis-tence, vile and evil-smelling. The cause of the stench is the great quantity of fish which is brought there, as well as the blood of the camels which are slaughtered in the streets. When we were there, we preferred to spend the night on board, although the sea was rough, rather than in the town, on account of its unpleasantness.

From there we sailed fifteen nights and arrived at Mogadishu, which is a very large town. The people have very many camels, and slaughter many hundreds every day. They have also many sheep. The merchants are wealthy, and manufacture a material which takes its name from the town and which is exported to Egypt and elsewhere.

Among the customs of the people of this town is the following: when a ship comes into port, it is boarded from *sanbuqs*, that is to say, lit-tle boats. Each *sanbuq* carries a crowd of young men, each carrying a covered dish, containing food. Each one of them presents his dish to a merchant on board, and calls out: "This man is my guest." And his fellows do the same. Not one of the merchants disembarks except to go to the house of his host among the young men,

save frequent visitors to the country. In such a case they go where they like. When a merchant has settled in his host's house, the latter sells for him what he has brought and makes his purchases for him. Buying anything from a merchant below its market price or selling him anything except in his host's presence is disapproved of by the people of Mogadishu. They find it of advantage to keep to this rule.

When the young men came on board the ship on which I was, one of them approached me. My companions said to him: "He is not one of the merchants: he is a lawyer." Then the young men called his companions and said: "This man is a guest of the Qadi [a local judge]." One of the Qadi's friends came among them, and he told him of this. The Qadi came down to the beach with some of his pupils and sent one on board to fetch me. Then I disem-barked with my companions, and greeted the Qadi and his followers. He said to me: "In the name of God, let us go and greet the Shaikh." "Who is the Shaikh?" I asked, and he replied: "The Sultan." For it is custom here to call the Sultan "Shaikh." I answered the Qadi: "I will visit him as soon as I have found lodging." He replied: "It is the custom here, whenever a lawyer, or a Sharif or holy man comes, that he should not go to his lodging until he has seen the Sultan." So I did what I was asked in accordance with their custom. . . .

We went to the chief mosque, and prayed behind the *maqsurah*, the enclosure for the Shaikh. When he came out of the *maqsurah*, I greeted him with the Qadi. He replied with his good wishes for us both, and talked to the Qadi in the local language, and then said to me in

PRIMARY SOURCE READING 7

Arabic: "You are welcome: you have honoured our country by coming and have rejoiced us." He went out into the courtyard of the mosque and stopped at the tomb of his son, which is there. He recited a passage from the [Quran] and prayed. Then came the wazirs [ministers], the amirs [local rulers] and military commanders and greeted him. In doing this they observed the same customs as are followed in the Yemen. The man who gives his greeting places his forefinger on the ground, and then on his head, and says: "May God make you glorious!"

INTERPRETING THE READING

Directions *Use the information from the reading to answer the following questions. If necessary, use a separate sheet of paper.*

1. Compare the lifestyles of the inhabitants of Zeila and Mogadishu.

_____

_____

_____

_____

2. According to the author, what are the religions of Zeila and Mogadishu? How does the Sultan's practice of the religion in Mogadishu differ from that of the people of Zeila?

_____

_____

_____

Critical Thinking

3. Making Inferences Why did the people of Mogadishu disapprove of a person "buying anything from a merchant below its market price or selling him anything except in his host's presence" and what advantages did it bring them?

_____

_____

_____

4. Recognizing Bias In what ways does the author reflect his bias regarding the people of Zeila and the people of Mogadishu?

_____

_____

_____

Reteaching Activity 7

Early African Civilizations

African civilizations came into early contact with one another through trade. The African continent is rich in natural resources. The great African kingdoms often traded resources for other products or for resources that they could not obtain or make themselves.

DIRECTIONS: The diagram below lists the major African kingdoms. Copy it onto a separate sheet of paper, filling in the boxes to show trading partners and the products they exchanged. Use the lists provided (some of the partners and products will appear more than once).

Trade Among African Civilizations				
Trading Partners		**Products Exchanged**		
Arabia	Persia	animal products	iron	olive oil
		copper	ivory	salt
Egypt	Rome	ebony	luxury goods	slaves
		frankincense	metal goods	textiles
India		gold	myrrh	wine

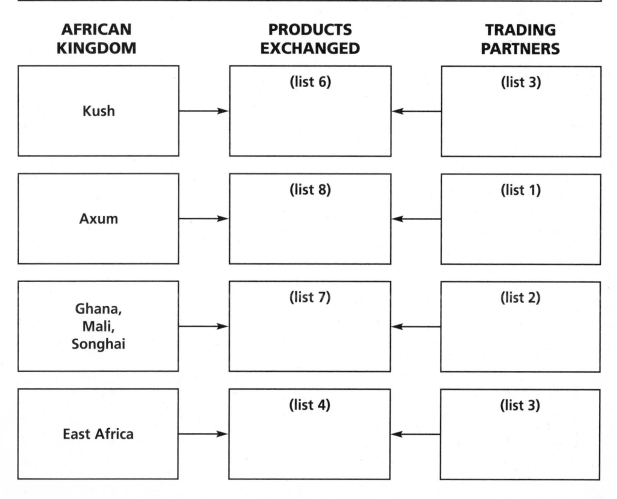

AFRICAN KINGDOM	PRODUCTS EXCHANGED	TRADING PARTNERS
Kush	(list 6)	(list 3)
Axum	(list 8)	(list 1)
Ghana, Mali, Songhai	(list 7)	(list 2)
East Africa	(list 4)	(list 3)

★ Enrichment Activity 7

Planning and Describing Migrations

Chapter 7 describes the developments of African civilizations over a period of 3,500 years. These civilizations flourished as they experienced migrations, cultural diffusion, and innovation. Contact with other cultures came about through trade, war, and travel.

> The Bantu people migrated from West Africa because the land they lived on grew less and less productive while the population continued to increase. The land was no longer able to support them, so many families decided to move in search of more space and better land. The Bantu migrations eventually carried people to the other side of the continent.

DIRECTIONS: Answer the questions below in the space provided.

1. Imagine that you are living in a Bantu village and are a member of the village council. Food production seems to be decreasing each year and the council is meeting to discuss the food shortage problem. Write a brief speech in which you outline your arguments to the council surrounding this issue. Ask yourself: Is it a temporary problem? Can new farming techniques be developed? Can the farmland be redistributed so that more arable land can be used for farming? Should the village move? Should only a few families move? Do you want to move from a village where you have lived your entire life?

   _____

   _____

   _____

   _____

2. In the end, the village council has decided that the only solution is to move to a new area. Develop a written plan for the village's migration. Start by thinking about the problems you will face. Where will you go? How will you get there? How will you protect yourselves?

   _____

   _____

   _____

   _____

3. Migrations still take place today around the world. Individuals and families decide to migrate from where they live for reasons other than just food and overpopulation. On a separate sheet of paper, write an essay describing various reasons you think people decide to move or migrate. Support your ideas with details or examples you have heard or read about in the news. Keep in mind that a migration may take place within one's own country or to another country.

CHAPTER 7

World Art and Music Activity 7

The Music of Africa

Although evidence suggests that music existed in Africa as far back as the 1900s B.C., a formal study of African music did not begin until the A.D. 1900s—a gap of nearly 4,000 years. What influences shaped African music during all those years?

DIRECTIONS: Read the passage below. Then answer the questions in the space provided.

Over the centuries, the rest of the world learned very little about the music of Africa because the cultures of the many countries that make up the continent have not been written, but oral. Until the invention of sound recording at the beginning of the 1900s, Africa's musical traditions were known only to those who had cultural ties to Africa. However, since the early 1900s, scholars have begun recording, analyzing, and writing about Africa's diverse musical culture.

North African culture includes elements that reflect its exposure to outside influence, as travelers and armies from Arabia and southern Europe visited and invaded the continent. Southwest Asian instruments such as lutes, flutes, and harps have been incorporated with the drums, bells, rattles, and other percussion instruments that pervade the music from this region. The music of southern Africa, in contrast, has had much less exposure to outside influences—song, dance, and drums are its main elements. In West Africa, Liberia, and the Congo, there is a greater proportion of flutes and bells, and various types of xylophones are common. Vocal music and dance are the chief means of musical expression.

Percussion instruments are found throughout the continent. Most are struck with the hand or a stick to produce their sound. They include drums, keyboard instruments such as the xylophone and the piano, and bells and chimes. Clapping hands, stamping feet, and snapping fingers also serve as percussion in musical performance. In Western music, percussion as provided by drums is generally considered to provide rhythm and nothing more. In Africa, however, a percussion rhythm is considered a melody in its own right. The drumbeats accompanying a song are not just keeping time; they are providing a counterpoint, or a second melody, to play against the one being sung.

African music relies heavily on instruments people make themselves out of available materials—bamboo flutes, ivory trumpets, drums made out of gourds, and rattles made of pebbles inside a container. Instruments had to be portable because so many African peoples moved from place to place in search of fresh food supplies and farmland.

African music from all regions is a part of everyday life—as central as eating or sleeping. A Tuareg herder of North Africa calls to livestock on a flute. Song and dance are essential elements of any religious ceremony; in certain kinds of ceremonies, Africans believe that spirits enter the bodies of the

Horn player, Benin

(continued)

> # World Art and Music Activity **7**

singers and dancers and express their wishes through these human mediums. Traditionally, song and drumbeats have been used as methods of communication over distance. Music also acts as a form of oral history, passing down stories and legends from one generation to the next.

Reviewing the Selection

1. Name some of the key instruments used to create African music.

   _____

   _____

2. Why was the music of the African continent not studied until the twentieth century?

   _____

   _____

3. What is one factor that accounts for the differences between northern and southern African music?

   _____

   _____

   _____

Critical Thinking

4. **Making Inferences** Why do you think African music, of all regions, relied so much on percussion instruments, song, and dance?

   _____

   _____

   _____

5. **Making Comparisons** Compare the use of percussion in Western music and African music.

   _____

   _____

   _____

6. **Drawing Conclusions** What role does music play within African cultures?

   _____

   _____

   _____

Chapter 7
Section Resources

SECTIONS

Guided Reading Activity 7-1

The Development of Civilizations in Africa

DIRECTIONS: Answer the following questions as you read Section 1.

1. Which continent is larger than the continent of Africa?

_____

2. What is distinctive about the Sahara?

_____

3. Describe the area known as the hump of Africa.

_____

4. Identify and describe a distinctive feature of the terrain far to the east in Africa.

_____

5. Name the four distinct climate zones in Africa.

_____

_____

6. Why were the Assyrians able to drive the Kushites out of Egypt and back to the upper Nile valley?

_____

_____

7. What were the characteristics of the state of Axum as it emerged?

_____

8. What significant event took place in the life of King Ezana of Axum in A.D. 324?

_____

_____

9. What effect did King Ezana's conversion have on Axum?

_____

10. When Arab forces took control of Egypt in 641, what then followed?

_____

11. Describe relations between Christian Axum and its Muslim neighbors.

_____

12. What expanding conflict deepened by the early fifteenth century, involving Axum?

_____

SECTION 7-1

Guided Reading Activity 7-2

Kingdoms and States of Africa

DIRECTIONS: As you are reading the section, decide if a statement is true or false. Write **T** if the statement is true or **F** if the statement is false. For all false statements write a corrected statement.

_____ **1.** The first of the great trading states to emerge in the area south of the Sahara was Ghana.

_____

_____ **2.** The kings of Ghana were strong rulers who governed with an elaborate system of laws.

_____

_____ **3.** The kingdom of Ghana prospered from its possession of both ivory and diamonds.

_____

_____ **4.** Salt, highly prized among the Ghanaians, was used to preserve food as well as to improve the taste of food.

_____

_____ **5.** Mali, established by Sundiata Keita, was the greatest of the new trading societies to replace Ghana in West Africa.

_____

_____ **6.** Once Mansa Musa felt secure in his rule, he decided as a devout Christian to make a pilgrimage to Makkah.

_____

_____ **7.** Two of Sunni Ali's conquests, Timbuktu and Jenne, were especially important as they gave Songhai control of the river valleys.

_____

_____ **8.** On the eastern fringe of the continent, the Bantu-speaking peoples gradually began to take part in trade up and down the East African coast.

_____

_____ **9.** As time passed, a mixed African-Arabian culture, eventually known as Swahili, began to emerge throughout the coastal area.

_____

_____ **10.** To build the walls of Great Zimbabwe, the granite blocks were laid with much mortar.

_____

Guided Reading Activity 7-3

African Society and Culture

DIRECTIONS: Fill in the blanks below as you read Section 3.

I. In Africa, the _____ between king and common people was not great.

   A. Often, the ruler would hold an audience to allow people to voice

   _____.

   B. _____ received favors from the king; the king received

   _____ from the merchants.

II. Sense of African _____ was determined by membership in an extended

   family and a _____ group.

   A. In some communities, women were _____.

   B. Both boys and girls were raised by their _____ until age six.

III. Slavery did not begin with the coming of the _____.

   A. Slavery had been practiced in Africa since _____ times.

   B. _____ regularly raided _____ south of the Sahara for

   captives.

IV. Most African societies _____ a belief in a _____

   creator god.

   A. The _____ people of Ghana believed in a supreme being called

   Nyame.

   B. One way to communicate with the gods was through _____.

V. The earliest art forms in Africa were _____.

   A. Carvings were believed to embody the _____ of the gods, spirits, and

   ancestors they represented.

   B. The _____ culture is the oldest known culture in West Africa to have

   created _____.

   C. African music and dance often served a _____ purpose.

Glencoe

WORLD HISTORY

Chapter 8 Resources
The Asian World, 400–1500

♪♭ Vocabulary Activity 8

The Asian World, 400–1500

DIRECTIONS: Select and write the term that best completes each sentence.

1. In the Chinese society, the _____ (scholar-gentry/archipelago) was considered to be the political and economic elite.

2. In marriage, a girl's parents were expected to provide a _____ (daimyo/dowry) to her husband.

3. After Genghis Khan died, his once-united empire was split into separate territories called _____ (khanates/savannas).

4. An accomplishment of the Tang dynasty was in the field of ceramics and the perfected making of _____ (porcelain/bronze).

5. _____ (Mandarins/Samurai) were Japanese warriors who swore to uphold Bushido and fight bravely.

6. Although the Japanese emperor supposedly was the paramount leader of Japan, in reality his power was gradually eroded by powerful Japanese warlords known as _____ (shoguns/daimyo).

7. Among the followers of Buddhism in India, one group believed that they were following the original teachings of the Buddha and called themselves the school of _____ (Mahayana/Theravada).

8. Less strict, the school known as _____ (Mahayana/Theravada) stressed the view that nirvana could be achieved through devotion to the Buddha.

9. Any large group of islands located close to one another, like the Florida Keys or the Philippine Islands, is called a(n) _____ (archipelago/shogunate).

10. As _____ (agricultural societies/trading societies), Southeast Asian states such as Srivijaya and the Sultanate of Melaka supported themselves chiefly through trade.

11. _____ (Bushido/Shinto) directed the lives of the samurai.

12. _____ (Zen/Shinto) is the state religion of Japan and considers the emperor divine.

13. The _____ (Bushido/Zen) sect of Buddhism defines different ways to achieve enlightenment.

Skills Reinforcement Activity 8

Identifying Central Issues

The ability to identify central issues in any work is critical to understanding it. To identify the key themes or ideas in a work like a book or a movie, begin by determining the setting and purpose. Ask what the work is about. Find the main idea of the work by identifying the focus or central issue.

DIRECTIONS: The passage below contains excerpts from the Japanese constitution prepared by the Japanese emperor Prince Shotoku. Read the passage and answer the questions that follow in the space provided.

I. Harmony is to be valued, and an avoidance of wanton opposition to be honored. All men are influenced by partisanship, and there are few who are intelligent. Hence there are some who disobey their lords and fathers, or who maintain feuds with the neighboring villages. But when those above are harmonious and those below are friendly, and there is concord in the discussion of business, right views of things spontaneously gain acceptance. Then what is there which cannot be accomplished?

II. Sincerely reverence the three treasures. The three treasures, viz. Buddha, the Law, and the Monastic orders . . . are the supreme objects of faith in all countries. Few men are utterly bad. They may be taught to follow it. But if they do not betake them to the three treas-ures, wherewithal shall their crooked-ness be made straight?

III. When you receive the imperial commands, fail not scrupulously to obey them. The lord is Heaven, the vassal is Earth. Heaven overspreads, and Earth upbears. When this is so, the four seasons follow their due course, and the powers of Nature obtain their efficacy. If the Earth attempted to overspread, Heaven would simply fall in ruin. Therefore is it that when the lord speaks, the vassal listens; when the superior acts, the inferior yields compliance. Consequently when you receive the imperial commands, fail not to carry them out scrupulously. Let there be a want of care in this matter, and ruin is the natural consequence.

1. What ideas are presented about Confucianism, Buddhism, and Chinese traditions?

_____

_____

2. What central issues can you identify?

_____

_____

3. List the quotes from the document that support the central issue.

_____

_____

Critical Thinking Skills Activity 8 | Identifying the Main Idea

When collecting data about a subject, look for patterns that organize the data into an understandable, and thus valuable, form. To find the main idea of a chart, graph, or table, look for a pattern—such as an increase or decrease—over time.

The climate throughout much of Asia is determined by how much rainfall an area gets. Seasons are often heralded by either monsoons—bouts of prolonged, heavy rainfall—or relatively dry weather.

DIRECTIONS: Look at the chart below of the monthly rainfall and temperature for three cities in Southeast Asia. Then answer the questions that follow.

Southeast Asia: Temperature (C°) and Monthly Rainfall (mm)		Jan	Feb	Mar	Apr	May	Jun	Jul	Aug	Sep	Oct	Nov	Dec
Sittwe	°C	21	22.5	26	28.5	29	28	27	27	27.5	27.5	25.5	22
	mm	3	5	13	50	348	1255	1364	1080	625	294	127	15
Yangon	°C	25	26	29	30.5	29	27	26.5	26.5	27	27.5	26.5	25
	mm	5	5	7	35	307	467	546	500	381	178	71	7
Saigon	°C	26	27	29	29.5	29	28	27	28	27	27	26.5	26
	mm	17	2	15	48	221	333	307	282	343	272	114	63

1. Based on the data, approximately when do the monsoon rains fall in all three locations? How much rain on average falls on each location during this season?

   _____

   _____

2. When does the hot season occur in the three areas mentioned in the chart? What is the relationship between the cycle of the hot seasons and the monsoons?

   _____

   _____

3. From looking at the chart, how could the monsoon cycles be used as a sort of calendar to help farmers plan their plantings and harvests?

   _____

   _____

4. Many countries in Asia, from India to Vietnam, have depended for centuries on the monsoon rains. Based on the information in the chart, why would a poor wet season— one that brings little rainfall—be a disaster for people?

   _____

★ HISTORY AND GEOGRAPHY ACTIVITY 8

Monsoons of India

Across the arid plains of northern India, hot dry winds send grit and dust flying, blackening the sky. Soon the monsoon will arrive. Until then, tension is high as the temperature and the winds continue to rise. How does the extreme nature of the monsoons affect India?

Monsoons are seasonal winds that change direction twice a year. The word *monsoon* is derived from the Arabic *mausim,* meaning "season." In Asia, a summer, or southwest, monsoon blows from mid-May through September and brings heavy rains from tropical oceans. A winter, or northeast, monsoon is a wind in the reverse direction, which begins during October and brings cool, dry, continental air.

For rural India, the arrival of the monsoon signifies the renewal of life. The monsoon can mean survival itself for farmers, since half of India's arable land depends solely on monsoon rains and a single growing season. When the monsoon is delayed, drought and famine can affect millions of people. Food prices then soar, causing inflation. Urban life can also be complicated by a delay in the arrival of the monsoon. About half of India's electricity is generated by hydropower and thus by the monsoons. While the monsoon can sometimes skip entire regions, a particularly harsh downpour can bring cyclones and floods to low-lying coastlines.

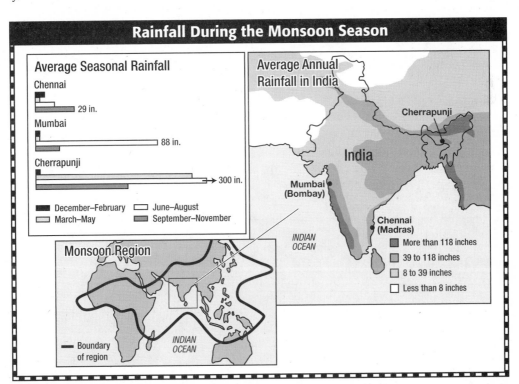

Asian agriculture and the survival of half the world's 5.5 billion people depend on the arrival of the monsoon, one of the most massive—and unpredictable—weather systems in the world. Late rains can have far-reaching economic, political, and social consequences in India.

73

HISTORY AND GEOGRAPHY ACTIVITY 8 (continued)

You can describe a place by its physical and human characteristics. Physical characteristics include climate, landforms, water forms, vegetation, and animal life. Monsoons are a distinguishing physical characteristic of India. A cycle of air set in motion by temperature differences over land and sea produces the monsoon season, which in turn affects other aspects of the nation's physical environment. Erosion of land, for example, is a significant result of monsoons, in which topsoil is washed away to sea. Exposed earth, especially in the mountains, cannot withstand the downpours of the monsoon, leading to devastation of the physical environment with dangerous landslides and loss of vegetation.

APPLYING GEOGRAPHY TO HISTORY

DIRECTIONS: Answer the questions below in the space provided.

1. What are some physical characteristics that describe a place?

   _____

2. Describe India's monsoon season.

   _____

3. How would a delay in the arrival of the monsoon affect rural and urban Indians?

   _____

   _____

Critical Thinking

4. **Predicting Consequences** Monsoon forecasts have been called the most important predictions in the world, yet the onset of the monsoon rains cannot be accurately predicted more than a few days in advance. Why are these forecasts so crucial? How do you think these forecasts affect people in India?

   _____

   _____

5. **Making Inferences** Why would Indians perceive rain and clouds differently from people in the West?

   _____

   _____

Activity

6. With your classmates, brainstorm a list of seasonal changes in climate in the United States. How do these changes affect physical and human environments in different parts of the country during the year?

Mapping History Activity 8

Languages of East and Southeast Asia

Throughout East and Southeast Asia, hundreds of languages are spoken by diverse groups of people. Such diversity can often be confusing to historians seeking the origins of various ethnic groups. However, scientists known as linguists look for similarities in the grammar and vocabulary of different languages to determine which ethnic groups are related. So far, linguists have identified at least five distinct language families, or languages that share similar structures and vocabulary, among Asian peoples. Observing how similar languages spread can give historians valuable insight into the interaction and movement of different ethnic groups.

DIRECTIONS: The map below shows East and Southeast Asia. Use the map to answer the questions and complete the activities that follow.

1. Label the major Asian language families listed below on the corresponding areas of the map.

   Sinitic: China and most of Southeast Asia

   Altaic: Mongolia, Central Asia, Korea, Japan

   Austronesian: Malay and Indonesia

   Indo-European: India

   Khmer: Cambodia

2. Identify the language family spoken in each of the following cities.

   Borobudur _____

   Nara _____

3. There are more than 20,000 islands in the Philippine and Indonesian archipelagos. How do you think the Austronesian language might have spread through this area?

   _____

   _____

4. What do you believe led to the development of so many different languages in Southeast Asia?

   _____

   _____

CHAPTER 8

Historical Significance Activity 8

Religion and State

Islam was the driving force behind many nationalist movements in the Middle East and also led to a split within the Indian nationalist movement. Considering that the Quran was written more than 1,300 years ago, how does one explain the continued influence and success of Islam? One possible explanation is that Islam is not only a religious tradition but, as the passage below indicates, it also provides explicit laws that help to form the economic "lifeblood" of Muslim nations.

Islam is acutely aware of life's material supports, and moved in on this area with laws that broke the barriers of economic caste and enormously reduced the injustices of special interest groups.

A comparison with the body's circulatory system can suggest how those laws proceed. Health requires that the body's blood flow freely and vigorously; sluggishness can induce disease, and blood clots occasion death. It is not different with the body politic where wealth takes the place of blood as the life-giving substance. As long as this analogy is honored and laws are in place to insure that wealth is in vigorous circulation, Islam does not object to the profit motive, economic competition, or entrepreneurial initiatives. So freely are these allowed, in fact, that the [Quran] has been characterized as "a manual for businessmen." It insists, though, that acquisitiveness and competition be balanced by the fair play that "keeps arteries open," and by compassion that is strong enough to pump life-giving blood—material resources—into its smallest capillaries. These "capillaries" are fed by the Poor Due which stipulates that annually a portion of one's holdings be distributed to the poor. As for the way to prevent "clotting," the [Quran] went after the severest economic curse of the day—primogeniture [exclusive right of inheritance by eldest son]—and outlawed it. It requires that inheritance be shared by all heirs, daughters included.

One verse in the [Quran] prohibits the taking of interest. At the time this was appropriate, for loans were then used to tide the unfortunate over in times of disaster. Now that loans provide venture capital, Muslims accommodate by involving lenders as partners in the venture and entitled thereby to a share of its profits. When capitalism is approached in this manner, Muslims consider it compatible with [Quranic] principles. Its excesses are another matter. The equalizing provisos [conditions] of the [Quran] would, if duly applied, offset them.

—From *The Illustrated World's Religions: A Guide to our Wisdom Traditions* by Huston Smith

DIRECTIONS: Answer the following questions on a separate sheet of paper.

1. How does the Quran circulate the economic "blood" of Islamic states?

2. What specific Islamic economic laws are mentioned in the passage?

★ **Cooperative Learning Activity 8** ★

A Civil Service Exam

BACKGROUND

During the Tang and Song dynasties in China, a person had to pass a civil service examination to earn a government job within the civilian bureaucracy. Before the civil service system was developed, appointments were based on favoritism and nepotism. The civil service system ensured that, for the most part, only the best-qualified people were hired to help run the government. By working as a group to create your own civil service examination, you will develop a better understanding of how civil service exams work and how they can be used to find the most qualified individuals to fill government jobs.

GROUP DIRECTIONS

1. Make sure everyone in the group understands what the federal civil service is (the nonelected roles and jobs within government-operated branches, departments, and agencies that support the functions of a government). Consider the types of jobs that exist in modern civil service (immigration officers, records clerks, legislative assistants, support staffs for various government offices such as agriculture, education, the Pentagon, and so on).

2. Brainstorm areas such as history, geography, civics, communication skills, and so on that you think might be useful on a civil service examination.

3. Create a set of 20 questions that you collectively believe could be included on a modern civil service examination and, for each question, identify an area of study that someone wanting to enter the civil service would want to know about.

4. Decide which questions would be most important to the examination. Create a list of 20 prioritized questions and exchange them with another group.

ORGANIZING THE GROUP

1. **Group Work/Decision Making** As a group, brainstorm the types of jobs that might have existed in the Tang and Song dynasty bureaucracies. What aspects of the central government functions would need support workers? Then identify similar or more modern jobs that would exist in the federal civil service of the United States today.

2. **Group Work** Collaboratively decide upon a list of areas that a civil service candidate should have more than a general knowledge about. List the areas in a place where the entire group can see them. Then brainstorm specific questions that would address these various areas. A recorder will need to be appointed to keep track of the group's ideas, probably on a flipchart or some other easily viewable group notes area. The area of knowledge should be noted beside each question.

Cooperative Learning Activity 8 (continued)

3. **Group Work/Decision Making** Identify the group's 20 best questions, using some form of group consensus-achieving mechanism or tabulation process. For example, each member of the group may pick her or his 20 favorites from the total list. By tallying the results from all group members, the group could arrive at the collective top 20 questions to be used for the examination. The group could then review the final selections to ensure that all areas of knowledge are appropriately represented.

4. **Individual Work** As individuals, write brief explanations of why you think the U.S. government should or should not use civil service examinations to screen candidates for support jobs in the federal government. Group members should consider the advantages and disadvantages of such a system. Present your explanations to the group and be prepared to defend your position.

5. **Extended Group Work** Have group members investigate what civil service jobs at the state or federal level require civil service examinations. If possible, obtain copies of previously given civil service examinations or practice examinations to share with the group and the class.

6. **Extended Group Work/Sharing** Trade lists of questions with another group, answer them as a team, and identify what your group thinks are the best or most appropriate questions on the other team's list.

GROUP PROCESS QUESTIONS

- What is the most important thing you learned about the civil service from this activity?

- What part of the project did you enjoy most?

- What questions did the other team create that were similar to your own group's questions? Which of the other team's questions were unlike any that your own group composed? Which were better than some of your own team's questions?

- Were any of your own group's questions too challenging to be used on a civil service exam or would any of them be unfair to exam-takers? Why?

Quick CHECK ✔

1. Was the goal of the assignment clear at all times?

_____

_____

2. How was creating examination questions different from other types of projects?

_____

_____

HISTORY SIMULATION ACTIVITY 8

Territorial Tracks

Geography played an important role in the development of the early civilizations of Asia. The people of Southeast Asia relied on the rivers that flow through their countries to grow and transport crops. The people of India relied on their rivers for trade with Southwest and East Asia. China, Korea, and Japan benefited from the geographic barriers of mountains and seas that isolated them from invasion.

TEACHER MATERIAL

Learning Objective To learn about the physical geography of China, Southeast Asia, Korea and Japan, and India.

Activity Four teams develop game materials using maps, atlases, and information from this chapter as well as geographic information about India from Chapter 3. Assign a specific country to each team. Team members write clues and answers about the landforms, waterways, climate, and cities of their assigned country, then play a geography game.

Teacher Preparation Make a copy of the handout material for each team. Gather the following supplies: a large wall map of Asia; four atlases; pushpins with red, green, blue, and yellow plastic heads; scissors; and a container for the clues (shoe box or paper bag).

Activity Guidelines

1. Explain to students that they are going to develop clues for a game based on geographic facts about the Asian countries in this chapter. Advise them to review the beginning of Chapter 3, which discusses the land of India.

2. Organize the class into four teams. Assign China to one team, Japan and Korea to another, India to a third, and Southeast Asia to the fourth. Give each team a copy of the handout material; scissors; an atlas; and a set of red, green, blue, or yellow pushpins.

3. Ask each team to choose a recorder. Then have each team work together to develop 10 clues with answers that describe the landforms, waterways, climate, and cities of their country. Each member then cuts out one or two clue cards, folds them, and places them in the single container provided for all clues.

4. Allow approximately half of the class period for teams to make the clue cards. When all cards are in the container, begin the game.

5. One student from one team chooses a clue from the container, reads it, and allows anyone from any of the other teams to respond. The team that makes the first correct answer sends its representative to the wall map to mark the spot of the answer with a team pin. The person who answered correctly reads the next clue. The game continues in this manner until all clues have been read. The team with the most pins on the map wins.

6. Encourage team members to discuss clues before giving their answers.

HANDOUT MATERIAL

Territorial Tracks—Clue Sheet

Sample Clue:	**Answer:**
A city located on a harbor and facing the Yellow Sea	Seoul, Korea

Clue: _____

Answer:

Clue: _____

Answer:

Clue: _____

Answer:

Clue: _____

Answer:

Clue: _____

Answer:

Clue: _____

Answer:

Clue: _____

Answer:

Clue: _____

Answer:

Clue: _____

Answer:

Clue: _____

Answer:

Time Line Activity 8

The Asian World

DIRECTIONS: In the centuries covered by Chapter 8, the civilizations of East and South Asia saw the rise and fall of many dynasties. Some political events are listed on the time line below. Read the time line, then answer the questions that follow.

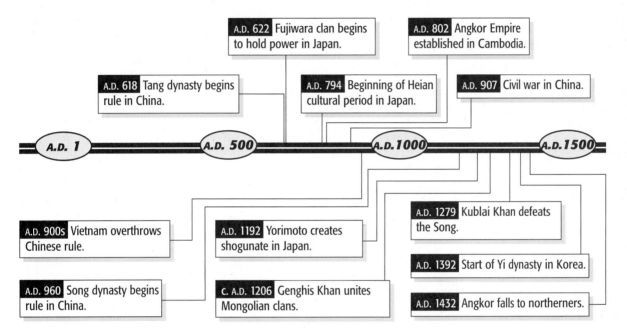

A.D. 622 Fujiwara clan begins to hold power in Japan.

A.D. 802 Angkor Empire established in Cambodia.

A.D. 618 Tang dynasty begins rule in China.

A.D. 794 Beginning of Heian cultural period in Japan.

A.D. 907 Civil war in China.

A.D. 900s Vietnam overthrows Chinese rule.

A.D. 1192 Yorimoto creates shogunate in Japan.

A.D. 1279 Kublai Khan defeats the Song.

A.D. 960 Song dynasty begins rule in China.

C. A.D. 1206 Genghis Khan unites Mongolian clans.

A.D. 1392 Start of Yi dynasty in Korea.

A.D. 1432 Angkor falls to northerners.

CHAPTER 8

1. In the first half of the A.D. 900s, which Asian countries experienced political changes?

   _____

2. When did Japan begin rule under a shogunate system?

   _____

3. How did Genghis Khan's unification of Mongolia influence later events in China?

   _____

4. How long did the kingdom of Angkor last?

   _____

5. Which kingdom was the last to establish a dynasty? What was the dynasty and when did it begin?

   _____

6. After China's civil war in A.D. 907, how many years passed before another Chinese dynasty was established?

   _____

Linking Past and Present Activity 8

Status of Women: Traditional China and Communist China

THEN Traditionally, Chinese women were considered to be intellectually inferior to men. The writings of Confucius include many disparaging remarks about the ability of women to learn.

Nonetheless, women in wealthy families were often well educated. Although some of them became poets and historians, these women were not allowed to take part in government unless they were members of the emperor's family. Poor women engaged in a variety of occupations, such as weaving, peddling, trading, and even construction work.

In many ways, a woman was almost completely under her husband's rule. However, her one source of power was the influence she had on her son. According to one famous story, it was the mother of the philosopher Mengzi who guided him to be a scholar.

Women were somewhat protected under the law. They were allowed to keep their dowries throughout marriage. Although husbands could easily divorce their wives for such reasons as disobedience, barrenness, illness, or jealousy, they could not do so if the wives had no place to go.

During the Song dynasty, the status of women declined. Their choice of occupations became severely limited. Most spent their lives as wives (or concubines) and mothers. In the Tang Era, having a wife with tiny feet became a status symbol. In response, parents bound their young daughters' feet in order to keep them from growing. This practice crippled most women for life, thus keeping them from being able to engage in productive work.

NOW In 1949 the Chinese Communists outlawed arranged marriages and made it illegal for men to have more than one wife. The government made schools co-educational, and female graduates were allowed to become government officials or enter a profession. Even women with little education were given the opportunity to hold a variety of jobs.

Tradition, however, continues to play a role in China. Some observers point out that ordinary Chinese women are still treated as domestic servants. Women who work as officials of Residents' Committees express pride in their responsibilities, which include inspecting the neighborhood for cleanliness, settling domestic quarrels, and organizing security patrols. However, these female officials complain that after working hard at their jobs, they still have to fulfill all of their traditional domestic duties.

Women with jobs in factories, schools, and hospitals are also responsible for taking care of their families. Most of these women work fewer hours than men in order to take care of their homes, and thus earn less money.

Some Chinese employers use the possibility that a woman might become a mother as an excuse for not hiring her for a better-paying position. They argue that a woman with children might find it too difficult to focus on work as opposed to her children. Other employers, when asked why women are not in managerial positions, simply reply, "It's always that way."

CRITICAL THINKING

Directions: Answer the following questions on a separate sheet of paper.
1. **Making inferences:** How does being unable to earn a living affect someone's freedom?
2. **Drawing conclusions:** What is one piece of evidence that at least some Chinese women of the past were intellectually gifted?

3. **Synthesizing information:** Point out a weakness in the argument that women don't make good managers because their duties as mothers interfere with their work. Do research in the library and on the Internet to learn why that argument is especially unsound when it comes to the working women of China. Write a brief report of your findings.

People in World History Activity 8   Profile 1

Su Dongpo (c. 1037–1101)

All I want is a son who is doltish and dumb. No setbacks or hardships will obstruct his path to the highest court posts.

Su Dongpo

Su Dongpo showed a passion for both politics and culture. He was a typical Confucian bureaucrat, who combined state business and the arts. A conservative, Su Dongpo led the opposition against reformers. He was imprisoned for slander, and then exiled to an area of China called Hubei.

Su Dongpo is most important for the lasting influence of his poems and essays. He is one of the Eight Prose Masters of the Tang and Song dynasties. His poetry is known for its natural, flowing style, a wide variety of subject matter, strong attention to detail, tenderness, playfulness, and humor. In a poem celebrating his son's first bath, he makes a biting political comment that is the quotation above.

In his essays Su Dongpo praises Confucian ideals of public service. Buddhist and Daoist ideas about change and the importance of non-attachment also impressed him. Two of his most influential essays dis-

cuss the shortness of life and the pleasure of drifting on a boat with friends, letting the current take them where it will.

Su Dongpo also brought poetry to his painting. In his writings he argues that painters should not so much represent how things look, but what they feel, as poets typically do.

Su Dongpo is also included among the Four Great Masters of calligraphy from the Song dynasty (960–1279). His scroll called *Red Cliff* especially inspired calligraphers of the Ming dynasty (1368–1644) and remains a masterwork to this day.

CHAPTER 8

REVIEWING THE PROFILE

Directions: Answer the following questions on a separate sheet of paper.

1. What ideas did Su Dongpo discuss in his essays?

2. What two areas of life did the typical Confucian bureaucrat combine?

3. What happened to Su Dongpo for opposing the reformers?

4. What are two qualities people ascribe to Su Dongpo's poetry?

5. **CRITICAL THINKING Making Generalizations.** Look at the paintings of four artists that you appreciate. Do you appreciate their work because they express their feelings or because these artists paint things as they appear? Do you agree with Su Dongpo that art should more express the artist's feelings? Be sure to give reasons for your answer.

> ## People in World History Activity 8
> ### Profile 2

Narasimhavarman I (ruled c. 625–645)

[This] is not simply a city made monumental by great temples and rich and varied innumerable minor ones; what rejoices me is to find the realization of an exceptionally well-grouped and comprehensive town plan.

A historian, commenting on the ancient city of Kanchi

Statue of Narasimhavarman I flanked by two noble-women, Adivaraha cave

In southeastern India, less than 50 miles (80 km) from the Indian Ocean, stands the city of Kanchipuram. Nearly 1,500 years ago, it was known as Kanchi, and it served as the capital of the great Pallava dynasty that ruled southern India for nearly 400 years. Narasimhavarman ruled the Pallava dynasty at its height.

The origins of the Pallava dynasty are obscure. Historians have deduced that the Pallavas were a pastoral people who lived in the far south of India. After they came to power and established their capital at Kanchi, they worked to extend their rule, fighting the many nearby competing kingdoms. For centuries the borders among these warring states were in constant flux. By about 550, however, the Pallavas were in firm control of southern India.

Narasimhavarman ascended to the throne in about 625. For decades, the Pallavas had been at war with the Chalukyas. At one point, Chalukya armies had advanced to within sight of the walls of Kanchi.

Narasimhavarman avenged these defeats. He led his armies into Chalukya territory, and captured and destroyed the Chalukya capital of Vatapi. Narasimhavarman was thereafter known as *Vatapikonde*, or "Taker of Vatapi." Thus, Narasimhavarman secured the power of the Pallavas.

Under Narasimhavarman, the people prospered. One visitor to Kanchi remarked on the expert cultivation of the rich soil in the region and on the admirable character of the people. Narasimhavarman founded new cities. Art and architecture also flourished, as Narasimhavarman commissioned fine sculptures and buildings that form a watershed in India's cultural history. It is through the inscriptions on many of these ancient rock creations that we have learned about Pallava. Only a century after their defeat at the hands of Narasimhavarman, the Chalukyas conquered the Pallavas.

REVIEWING THE PROFILE

Directions: Answer the following questions on a separate sheet of paper.

1. What was the capital of the Pallava dynasty?

2. What were Narasimhavarman's major accomplishments?

3. **Critical Thinking** Determining Relevance. Narasimhavarman lived more than 1,000 years ago and ruled a kingdom that no longer exists. Do you think it is important to learn about such historical figures? Explain.

PRIMARY SOURCE READING 8

Buddhism and Everyday Life

Buddhism spread quickly throughout southern and eastern Asia in the centuries following the Buddha's death. Monks and disciples from India taught the ethical and religious messages of the Buddha to people in China, Japan, and Korea. In time, disputes over the nature of the Buddha himself led to the separation of Buddhism into Theravada and Mahayana. The following excerpt is taken from a Theravada text, which viewed the Buddha not as a divine being but as an inspired human teacher.

Guided Reading *In this selection, read to learn how Buddha counseled his followers to lead virtuous lives.*

Once when the Lord [the Buddha] was staying in the Bamboo Grove at Rājagaha, Singāla, a householder's son, got up early, went out from Rājagaha, and, with his clothes and hair still wet from his morning ablutions [bathing], joined his hands in reverence and worshiped the several quarters of [the] earth and sky—east, south, west, north, above, and below. Now early that same morning the Lord dressed himself, and with bowl and robe went into Rājagaha to beg his food. He saw Singāla worshiping the quarters, and asked him why he did so.

"When my father lay dying," Singāla replied, "he told me to worship the quarters thus. I honor my father's words, and respect and revere them, and so I always get up early and worship the quarters in this way."

"But to worship the six quarters thus is not in accordance with noble conduct."

"How then, Sir, should they be worshiped in accordance with noble conduct? Will the Lord be so good as to tell me?"

"Listen then," said the Lord, "and I'll tell you. Mark well what I say!"

"I will, Sir," Singāla replied. And the Lord spoke as follows:

"If the noble lay-disciple has given up the four vices of action, if he does no evil deed from any of the four motives, if he doesn't follow the six ways of squandering his wealth, if he avoids all these fourteen evils—then he embraces the six quarters, he is ready for the conquest of both worlds, he is fortunate both in this world and the next, and when his body breaks up on his death he is reborn to bliss in heaven.

"What are the four vices of action that he gives up? They are injury to life, taking what is

not given, base conduct in sexual matters, and false speech. . . .

"What are the four motives of evil deeds which he avoids? Evil deeds are committed from partiality, enmity, stupidity, and fear.

"And what are the six ways of squandering wealth? They are addiction to drink, the cause of carelessness; roaming the streets at improper times; frequenting fairs; gambling; keeping bad company; and idleness. . . .

"There are four types who should be looked on as enemies in the guise of friends: a grasping man; a smooth-spoken man; a man who only says what you want to hear; and a man who helps you waste your money.

"The grasping man is an enemy on four grounds: he is grasping; when he gives a little he expects a lot in return; what duty he performs he does out of fear; and he only serves his own interests.

"The smooth-spoken man is an enemy on four grounds: he speaks you fair about the past; he speaks you fair about the future; he tries to win you over by empty promises; but when there's something to be done he shows his shortcomings.

"The man who only says what you want to hear is an enemy on four grounds: he consents to an evil deed; he doesn't consent to a good one; he praises you to your face; but he runs you down behind your back.

"The wastrel is an enemy on four grounds: he is your companion when you drink; when you roam the streets at improper times; when you go to fairs; and when you gamble.

"But there are four types who should be looked on as friends true of heart: a man who seeks to help you; a man who is the same in weal [well-being] and woe; a man who gives good advice; and a man who is sympathetic. . . .

> The friend who is a helper,
>   The friend in weal and woe,
> The friend who gives good counsel,
>   The friend who sympathizes—
> These the wise man should know
>   As his four true friends,
> And should devote himself to them
>   As a mother to the child of her body.

> The wise and moral man
>   Shines like a fire on a hilltop,
> Making money like the bee,
>   Who does not hurt the flower.
> Such a man makes his pile
>   As an anthill, gradually.
> The man grown wealthy thus
>   Can help his family
> And firmly bind his friends
>   To himself. He should divide
> His money in four parts;
>   On one part he should live,
> With two expand his trade,
>   And the fourth he should save
> Against a rainy day."

INTERPRETING THE READING

Directions *Use information from the reading to answer the following questions. If necessary, use a separate sheet of paper.*

1. What issue does Singāla ask the Buddha to help him clarify?

_____

_____

2. How does the Buddha answer Singāla?

_____

_____

3. What distinctions does the Buddha make between good men and enemies?

_____

_____

Critical Thinking

4. Making Inferences Based on this selection, why might the Buddha's teachings, especially those dealing with abstinence and saving money, be attractive to his followers?

_____

_____

5. Identifying Bias What evidence from this selection indicates that the Theravada viewed the Buddha as an inspired human teacher?

_____

_____

Name _____ Date _____ Class _____

The Asian World

Chinese culture changed with each succeeding Chinese dynasty. In many cases, political change (changing of dynasties) brought about innovation in other areas. Change has contributed to China's diverse and dynamic society, which, in turn, has contributed to religious, scientific, and artistic progress throughout the world.

DIRECTIONS: Fill in the blank spaces in the webs below, selecting the correct answers from the list provided. Parts of the webs have already been filled in.

- Daoism
- steel
- Neo-Confucianism
- landowners

- Song

- cotton
- fire-lance
- scholar-gentry
- invention of printing

- peasants

- girl's parents provide a dowry when she marries
- completed the Grand Canal
- restored the power of China in East Asia
- Indian religion brought to China by merchants and missionaries
- economic prosperity and cultural achievement

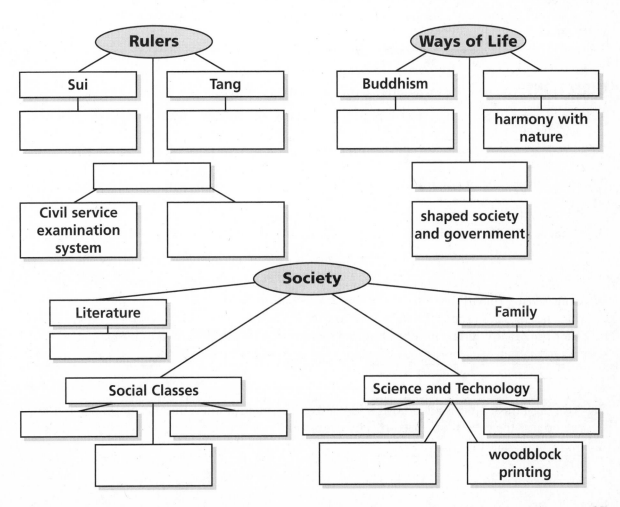

87

★ Enrichment Activity **8**

"Happy New Year!" Chinese Style

In the United States, we measure years officially by recording how long it takes for the earth to revolve once around the sun. This method is called a solar calendar, and it corresponds accurately with the seasons of the year. However, in order to calculate the solar year, a scientist needs instruments to measure the angle of the sun as it shines on the earth. Since many ancient cultures lacked these instruments, they relied on a lunar calendar instead.

A lunar calendar is based on the cycle of the moon's phases, which can be observed without the use of scientific instruments. According to the traditional Chinese calendar, the year is made up of 12 lunar months. A lunar month is about 29.5 days long. This is the time it takes for the moon to pass through a complete cycle of phases, from full moon to new moon to full moon.

A year made up of 12 lunar months is shorter than a solar year. After a few years, lunar and solar calendars are out of synchronization. To correct this, a "leap month" is periodically added to the Chinese lunar calendar. Even so, Chinese holidays do not fall on the same solar-calendar dates each year. For example, Chinese New Year can occur anytime between January 21 and February 19 on the solar calendar. By contrast, New Year's Day on the solar calendar is always January 1.

DIRECTIONS: Answer the questions below in the space provided.

1. What is the difference in length between a solar year (365 days) and a non-leap lunar year? _____
   _____

2. How long is an "average solar month," one-twelfth of a solar year? _____
   _____

3. What is the difference between the length of an "average solar month" and the length of a lunar month?_____
   _____

4. Considering this difference, how many lunar months would pass before the lunar calendar was 30 days (approximately a lunar month) behind the solar calendar? Based on this, after how many lunar months should a leap month be added to the lunar calendar?
   _____
   _____

5. Although the Chinese calendar is still used for calculating the timing of holidays, the solar calendar is the official one used by government and commerce. Why do you think this is so?
   _____
   _____

World Art and Music Activity 8

Chinese Porcelain

The best-known Chinese porcelain comes from the Song dynasty and consists primarily of blue designs on a white background. The Chinese first made porcelain in the A.D. 600s, during the Tang dynasty, and they perfected it throughout the Song and Yuan dynasties.

DIRECTIONS: Read the passage below about this ancient art. Then answer the questions in the space provided.

Porcelain is made of a white clay called *kaolin.* This substance is also referred to as china clay because it is found nowhere else in the world. After an object is shaped out of the clay, it is covered with a glaze and then fired in a very hot oven, called a kiln. The result is a hard object with a durable, glasslike surface.

Tang dynasty ceramics are noted for their beautiful shapes and the development of colored glazes. The pitchers, jars, bowls, and vases usually have strong, simple shapes—a round jar with a small lip, a bowl with slight indentations making it look like a flower, a round pitcher with a handle. These pleasing shapes are combined with a wide range of colors. Chinese artists used various minerals to produce black, blue, green, yellow, and creamy white glazes. Sometimes brown and white clay were mixed together and covered with a transparent glaze, producing a marbled effect.

Most pottery during the Tang dynasty was intended to be placed in tombs. Objects vary in size from toys and animal figures a few inches high to large horses and camels. Many depict soldiers and women on horseback, people dancing and playing a variety of musical instruments, and caricatures of foreigners from central and western Asia. The most extraordinary pieces are the tomb guardians, fierce armed men often standing on demons. They are minutely detailed and glazed in vibrant colors. Tomb ceramics were made cheaply and in bulk. They have been found in tombs of average people as well as those of royalty.

During the Song dynasty, Chinese travelers brought back cobalt from Southwest Asia. This blue

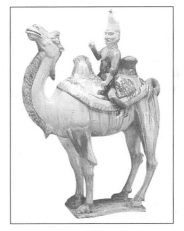

Porcelain figure of a rider on a camel

mineral was the impetus for the era of blue and white porcelain. The contrast between the pure white of the kaolin and the bright blue cobalt is striking. The designs were predominantly flowers, leaves, and vines, often in intricate patterns. Song porcelain was produced for the nobility, which may account for it being more elaborate than Tang wares. Song pieces have a wider range of colors and shapes, and the surface might be carved with various designs.

Song vessels were fired upside down, so the rims had to be left unglazed so they would not stick to the kiln. The rims were later covered in bronze or silver.

The rarest and most esteemed Song porcelain is called *Ju.* Instead of the typically bold Song colors, these delicate ceramics are glazed in lavender, pinkish-yellow, and pale turquoise, a color that has been described as "so subtle that it seems to be emitting light rather than reflecting it."

(continued)

World Art and Music Activity 8

The Yuan dynasty was a period of much innovation and experiment. Much of its porcelain was produced for export to Southwest Asia and North Africa. These ceramics are elaborate and consist of intricately carved dragons and phoenixes under colored glazes. Jars have lids with handles in the form of sculptured animals. In addition, auspicious words are included, such as *fu* ("happiness") and *shu* ("long life"). Many figures of gods and goddesses were produced and used in homes as shrines.

Reviewing the Selection

1. What is porcelain and how is it made?

_____

_____

_____

_____

Critical Thinking

2. Making Comparisons Briefly describe how Tang and Song pottery are similar and different.

_____

_____

_____

_____

_____

_____

_____

3. Predicting Consequences Porcelain of the Tang, Song, and Yuan dynasties shows a progression of style. Predict what the ceramics of the next dynasty, the Ming, were like.

_____

_____

_____

_____

_____

_____

_____

_____

Glencoe

WORLD HISTORY

Chapter 8
Section Resources

SECTIONS

Guided Reading Activity 8-1

China Reunified

DIRECTIONS: Answer the following questions as you read Section 1.

1. What was the most important accomplishment of the Sui dynasty in China?

_____

2. The completion of the Grand Canal linking the Huang He and Chang Jiang had an important effect on China. What was it?

_____

3. List two reforms instituted by the early rulers of the Tang dynasty.

_____

_____

4. The Song dynasty, which ruled from 960 to 1279, was noted for two positive achievements. Name them.

_____

5. What did the Song rulers do to stay in power?

_____

6. Describe the government of China from the beginning of the Sui dynasty to the end of the Song dynasty.

_____

_____

7. How was the Chinese economy affected during this same time period?

_____

8. Describe the effects of three new products, which came about through Chinese technology during the Tang dynasty.

_____

_____

_____

9. What products did the Chinese export, and what did they receive in return?

_____

10. What city became the wealthiest city in the world during the Tang Era?

_____

11. Female children in China were considered less desirable than male children. What customs practiced by the Chinese make this obvious?

_____

_____

SECTION 8-1

Guided Reading Activity 8-2

The Mongols and China

DIRECTIONS: As you are reading the section, decide if a statement is true or false. Write **T** if the statement is true or **F** if the statement is false. For all false statements write a corrected statement.

_____ **1.** The Mongols were a pastoral people from the region of modern-day Mongolia who were organized loosely into clans.

_____

_____ **2.** The Mongols ruled over one of the smaller empires in the history of the world.

_____

_____ **3.** Large walls and fortresses kept the Mongols from attacking western Europe.

_____

_____ **4.** Kublai Khan, who ruled China until his death in 1294, established his capital at "the city of the Khan," later known by the name Singapore.

_____

_____ **5.** Marco Polo of Italy visited China during the reign of Kublai Khan and was much impressed by the magnificent splendor of the capital city at Khanbaliq.

_____

_____ **6.** Zhu Yuanzhang, the son of a great king, put together an army in 1368, ended the Mongol dynasty, and set up the Ming dynasty.

_____

_____ **7.** Buddhism was brought to China in the first century A.D. by merchants and missionaries from India.

_____

_____ **8.** Neo-Confucianists believe only in the material world and that humans have no link whatsoever to a spiritual realm.

_____

_____ **9.** Chinese poems celebrated the glories of warfare and conquest.

_____

_____ **10.** Influenced by Daoism, Chinese artists went into the mountains to paint and find the Dao, or Way, in nature.

_____

SECTION 8-2

Guided Reading Activity 8-3

Early Japan and Korea

DIRECTIONS: Fill in the blanks below as you read Section 3.

Japan is a mountainous chain of **(1)** _____. Only about

(2) _____ percent of its total land area can be farmed. The ancestors

of present-day Japanese settled near the modern cities of **(3)** _____

and **(4)** _____ in the first centuries A.D. Their society was made up of

(5) _____. Eventually, one ruler of the **(6)** _____ clan

achieved supremacy over the others and became ruler of Japan.

In the early seventh century, **(7)** _____, a Yamato prince, tried to

unify the various clans. Taishi sent representatives to China to learn how the Chinese

organized their **(8)** _____. He then began to create a

(9) _____ government based on the Chinese model.

After Shotoku Taishi's death in 622, political power fell into the hands of the

(10) _____ clan. In 710, a new **(11)** _____ was estab-

lished at Nara. The emperor began to use the title **(12)** _____.

By 794, the government of Japan was returning to the earlier

(13) _____ system. With the decline of central power, local

(14) _____ tended to take justice into their own hands. A new class of

military servants called **(15)** _____ emerged, whose purpose was to

protect the security of their employers.

Spiritual beliefs known as **(16)** _____ evolved into a state doc-

trine linked to a belief in the **(17)** _____ of the emperor and the

sacredness of the **(18)** _____. Zen beliefs became part of the samurai

warrior's **(19)** _____.

The closeness of Korea to **(20)** _____ has greatly affected its his-

tory. No society in **(21)** _____ was more strongly influenced by the

Chinese model than Korea. The **(22)** _____ dynasty adopted Chinese

political institutions.

📖 Guided Reading Activity 8-4

India after the Guptas

DIRECTIONS: Fill in the blanks below as you read Section 4.

I. A split developed among followers of _____ in India.

   A. The school of _____ followed the original teachings of the Buddha.

   B. Mahayana Buddhism taught _____ as a true heaven.

II. _____ became popular in the northwestern corner of India.

   A. India was divided into about seventy states, which _____ constantly.

   B. Rebellious _____ slaves founded a new Islamic state called Ghazni.

III. During the 1380s, Timur Lenk conquered the region east of the _____.

   A. The _____ of Timur Lenk removed a menace from the various states of India.

   B. By the early _____, two new challenges had appeared.

      1. One was a newly emerging nomadic power from the north, _____.

      2. The other came from Europe, in the form of _____ traders arriving by sea.

IV. Muslim rulers in India viewed themselves as _____.

   A. They maintained _____ between Muslim rulers and the Hindus.

   B. Many Muslim rulers in India were _____ of other faiths.

   C. Overall, _____ marked the relationship between Muslim and Hindus.

V. From the eighth century on, Indian _____ built monumental Hindu temples.

   A. The greatest examples of Hindu temple art of this period are found at _____.

   B. One of the greatest masters of _____ was Dandin, a seventh-century author.

SECTION 8-4

Guided Reading Activity 8-5

Civilization in Southeast Asia

DIRECTIONS: Fill in the blanks below as you read Section 5.

1. Southeast Asia has two major _____ parts. One is the
   _____ region, extending from the Chinese border down to the tip of the
   Malay Peninsula and the other is an extensive chain of _____.

2. _____ and _____ often cut off people in mainland
   Southeast Asia from one another. These geographical barriers may help explain why
   Southeast Asia is one of the few regions in Asia that was never _____
   under a single government.

3. The _____ were one of the first peoples in Southeast Asia to develop
   their own state and their own culture. In spite of being conquered by China in 111 B.C.,
   the Vietnamese clung to their own _____.

4. In the ninth century, the kingdom of Angkor arose in the region that is present-day
   _____. Angkor faced enemies on all sides, and in 1432 the
   _____ from the north destroyed the Angkor capital.

5. The Thai first appeared in the sixth century as a _____ people in
   _____. Migrating southward, the Thai set up their own
   _____ on the Chao Phraya River.

6. The Burmans had migrated from the _____ of Tibet beginning in the
   seventh century A.D. The Burmans were _____ peoples, but they
   adopted farming soon after their arrival in Southeast Asia.

7. For centuries, the Malay world had been tied to the trade that passed from East Asia
   into the _____. Eventually, almost the entire population of the region
   was converted to _____.

8. Trade through Southeast Asia expanded after the emergence of _____ in
   the area and reached greater heights after the Muslim conquest of _____.

WORLD HISTORY

Chapter 9 Resources

Emerging Europe and the
Byzantine Empire, 400–1300

⟨NBC⟩ Vocabulary Activity 9

Emerging Europe and the Byzantine Empire, 400–1300

DIRECTIONS: Match each term with its definition by writing the correct letter on the blank.

A.	chivalry	**F.**	knight	**K.**	monk
B.	wergild	**G.**	estate	**L.**	pope
C.	abbess	**H.**	vassal	**M.**	feudalism
D.	clergy	**I.**	bishopric	**N.**	scriptoria
E.	schism	**J.**	monastery	**O.**	missionary

_____ **1.** value of a person in money

_____ **2.** the head of the Roman Catholic Church

_____ **3.** man who separates himself from human society to pursue dedication to God

_____ **4.** rooms in a monastery set aside for the writing of manuscripts and records

_____ **5.** political or social system based on the holding of all land in fief and the resulting relation of lord to vassal and characterized by homage and legal and military service of tenants

_____ **6.** system, principles, and customs of knighthood

_____ **7.** someone who goes out to spread a religious message

_____ **8.** major social class, such as the clergy, the nobility, or the commons, formerly possessing distinct political rights

_____ **9.** a separation or break

_____ **10.** church officials

_____ **11.** man who serves a lord in a military capacity

_____ **12.** the district over which the jurisdiction of a bishop extends

_____ **13.** a religious community where monks live a spiritual life

_____ **14.** female superior of a convent of nuns

_____ **15.** tenant giving military service as a mounted man-at-arms to a feudal landholder

Skills Reinforcement Activity 9

Distinguishing Between Fact and Opinion

Theodora, wife of Byzantine emperor Justinian I, was an unconventional woman—one who has attracted the attention of many historians and biographers. As questions about her life as an actress and then empress are debated, we hear a mixture of facts and opinions that attempt to explain her character and her importance in history. In order to evaluate these explanations, we must first know how to distinguish fact from opinion.

DIRECTIONS: Read the following passage, then answer the questions below in the space provided.

The Woman Behind the Man Shows Her Strength

Byzantine emperor Justinian was a strong and well-educated leader. It is surprising that a man of such importance would have married an actress, no matter how beautiful she was. Yet Theodora was more than beautiful. She was intelligent and understood government. She influenced the awarding of some positions and generously gave jobs to friends.

Theodora also took action on behalf of women, convincing Justinian to grant a woman the right to own land that equaled the value of any wealth that she had brought to the marriage. It was only fair that a woman be no less wealthy after her marriage than she had been before it. Without this right to property, some widows had been unable to support their children.

Theodora's greatest achievement was saving her husband's position as emperor. During a rebellion, several of the emperor's advisers wanted to leave the city. Theodora announced that she would not leave. Justinian was able to suppress the rebellion and remain in power.

1. Does the title of the article express a fact or an opinion? Why?

_____

2. a. List several facts from the article.

_____

_____

b. How do you know these are facts?

_____

3. Which individual words in this article suggest that an opinion is being expressed?

_____

4. In a sentence or two, sum up the main opinion that the writer is expressing.

_____

_____

CHAPTER 9

Critical Thinking Skills Activity 9 | Formulating Questions

In order to learn the most important information about a topic, you need to develop the skill of formulating good questions. When you are asked to write a report, for instance, you must be able to generate a list of pertinent questions your report will answer. Good questions not only guide your research but also add depth and interest to your work.

DIRECTIONS: Read the following research topics. Develop a list of questions that would be appropriate. Use the list of questions below for ideas, but make your own questions specific to the topic.

1. Early Eastern Slavs were mostly farmers who lived in small villages. Find out how they plowed the soil, planted their crops, and harvested their fields.

2. In 1215, King John of England placed his seal on the Magna Carta. Find out why the English nobles forced him to do this.

_____

Types of Questions to Ask Yourself Before You Begin Your Research:

- What am I being asked to do?
- Why is this topic important?
- Who are the important people involved?
- Where did the events take place?
- What is the time period? What are the dates?
- Why did the event happen? Is there an underlying reason for its occurrence?
- Could the events have occurred in a different manner?
- Can comparisons be drawn to other events?
- Can I/should I accept this information as true?

★ HISTORY AND GEOGRAPHY ACTIVITY 9

Vikings

Off the Northumbrian coast of north-eastern Britain sped long, low ships with high, curving prows and sterns. The ships rammed onto the undefended beaches of Lindisfarne—a lonely and windswept island, home only to the monks of St. Cuthbert's monastery. Fearsome, screaming warriors poured from the bellies of these great sailing vessels. What were the invaders seeking?

The warriors who attacked and raided St. Cuthbert's in A.D. 793 were skilled sailors, fierce fighters, and greedy looters. They wreaked havoc as they hacked their way into the monastery's chapels and store-rooms, looking for jewel-covered illumi-nated manuscripts, golden crucifixes, and silver communion vessels. Bloody raids followed in Britain and Ireland and, by the 840s, in France as well. So many churches

Siege of Paris

The town trembles, and horns resound, the walls are bathed in floods of tears, the whole region laments: from the river are heard the horn blasts. Stones and spears one on top of another fly through the air. Our men give a loud battle cry which is answered by the Danes. Suddenly the earth shakes (as a tower falls): our men lament, the Danes rejoice. Reinforcements fighting bravely try to reach those groaning in the tower; but in vain.

—Abbon's account of attack in A.D. 886

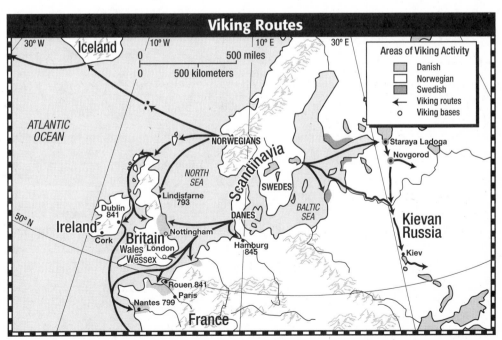

Viking activity in western Europe during the A.D. 800s reflected the warriors' interest in attaining wealth, land, and fame.

HISTORY AND GEOGRAPHY ACTIVITY 9 (continued)

and monasteries were robbed that a new prayer was added to the Christian litany: "From the fury of the Northmen, O Lord, deliver us."

Known as the Vikings, these fighting men—Scandinavians from Norway, Denmark, and Sweden—sought new sources of land, fame, and wealth. Vikings were attracted to areas throughout eastern and western Europe that offered luxury items such as gold and silver; a Nordic warrior's success in life was measured by his plunder. Vikings often buried their treasures. The contents of such hoards reflect Viking movement during the 800s and 900s. Nordic traders who traveled into Russia and met Arab traders, for instance, buried silver that had originated from the coinage

of the caliphate. Other hidden Viking treasures came from silver deposits that originated in Germany.

Few places in the world are entirely self-sufficient. Resources are often distributed unequally among areas and people. At times people move to new locations in order to meet their needs; at other times trade enables resources and products to be more equally distributed. Viking movement in Europe initially focused on trading and raiding. Over time, however, the Vikings changed their activities, from trading and raiding to conquest and settlement. Patterns of Viking movement—whether by trade, warfare, or settlement—established new networks of transportation and communication.

APPLYING GEOGRAPHY TO HISTORY

DIRECTIONS: Answer the questions below in the space provided.

1. Explain how the needs of certain groups can affect their movement.

   _____

2. Which factors influenced Viking movement?

   _____

3. Why do you think the Vikings traded with the Europeans and then turned to conquest and settlement?

   _____

   _____

Critical Thinking

4. **Drawing Conclusions** What do buried Viking treasures tell us about the warriors?

   _____

   _____

Activity

5. Organize a debate on the following topic: The Vikings sailed to North America before Christopher Columbus.

Mapping History Activity 9

Justinian's Conquests

After the Western Roman Empire fell following several waves of invasions, Constantinople became the new power center for the empire. Byzantine emperor Justinian wanted to recover the lands lost to the invaders and reconstitute the Roman Empire. In the end, Justinian was able to take back much, but not all, of the territory that had once belonged to Rome.

DIRECTIONS: The map below shows Justinian's Empire. Use the map to answer the questions and complete the activity that follow. Use a separate sheet of paper.

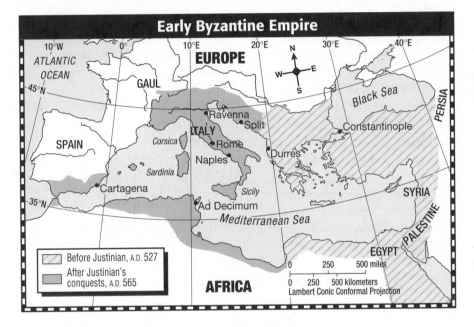

1. Constantinople is about how many miles from Rome?

2. Constantinople sits at the crossroads of which two bodies of water?

3. Read the following historical description of Justinian's campaigns to take back the lost territories. Using the information provided, draw arrows on the map to show the routes that were taken.

In A.D. 533, the first expedition left Constantinople and was directed toward Africa. The Byzantine forces led by Belisarius landed in what is today the country of Tunisia. There, they defeated the Vandals in a battle at Ad Decimum and at the nearby city of Tricamarum. From there, the Byzantines sailed to Sicily, Sardinia, and Corsica and took back those islands. In A.D. 535, the second expedition was launched. This time, the plan was to recapture the Italian Peninsula. Belisarius, who occupied the island of Sicily, landed at Naples, fought his way to Rome, and pushed north to Ravenna. At the same time, Mundus, operating on the Balkan Peninsula, launched an invasion from Durres to Split. A third expedition was led by Liberius in A.D. 554. He landed at Cartagena and fought the Visigoths to take back Spain. Despite these successes, Justinian's expanded empire failed to include the interior of Gaul (now called France) or Spain.

| Historical Significance Activity 9 |

History Repeats Itself

Events that we hear about in the news often have roots in the past, sometimes the distant past. An unresolved conflict can smolder for decades and then reignite, as this 1996 article shows.

Estonia Shakes Up the Orthodox Church

From Vladivostok to Corfu, Eastern Christians will celebrate Orthodoxy Sunday on March 2, 1996. This day commemorates the ninth-century ruling that allowed the veneration of icons. This ruling put an end to the efforts of earlier Byzantine emperors to stop the religious practice. This is the 1,153rd time this decision has been celebrated, and one might expect the Church to be long past divisions. Yet a new split may be developing.

This rift is between Bartholomew I, the 270th patriarch of Constantinople, and the powerful patriarchate of Moscow. The focus of the rift is the Estonian Church. The approximately 80 parishes of Estonia recently chose to be under the authority of Istanbul after belonging to the Moscow patriarchate for more than 50 years.

While Istanbul sees the change as the will of the majority of Estonians, Moscow does not. Russian president Boris Yeltsin told Estonia's president Lennart Meri that he was concerned about Russian-speaking Estonians who might not be well served by the change.

In fact, Yeltsin's concerns are as much political as they are religious. Both Yeltsin and Patriarch Alexy of Moscow are under pressure from Russian nationalists. The irony here is that Patriarch Alexy is from Estonia.

The tug-of-war over the Estonian parishes is a reminder of the shift in the center of eastern Christian religion. In 1510, the monk Filofey said, "Two Romes have fallen, but the third stands. . . ."

DIRECTIONS: Answer the following questions in the space provided.

1. The opening sentence mentions Vladivostok and Corfu to illustrate the span of the Eastern Orthodox world. Look up Vladivostok and Corfu in an atlas. What and where is each place?

   _____

2. **a.** According to the article, who are the two rivals?

   _____

   b. What is the conflict between them?

   _____

   _____

3. Identify the three Romes the monk Filofey referred to in the quote from 1510.

   _____

   _____

★ Cooperative Learning Activity **9** ★  ★

A Symbol of the Crusades

BACKGROUND

In medieval times, a warrior's shield made a statement about who he was, to what family he belonged, the identity of his lord, and his beliefs. Both European knights and foot soldiers used shields during the Crusades. In this activity, groups will design a shield for some famous person or event in the Crusades. The front of the shield will contain symbols that illustrate the person's life or the event. The back of the shield will describe the person or event selected and their or its significance in the Crusades. This activity will combine research skills and design skills to help you learn more about this period in history, Europe, the Byzantine Empire, and the Crusades.

GROUP DIRECTIONS

1. Use your textbook or other sources to decide on a person or event during the Crusades. Suggested topics or people include:

Pope Urban II	the First Crusade
the Third Crusade	Richard the Lionhearted
Saladin	the Fourth Crusade
the Children's Crusade	Alexius I
Nicholas of Cologne	

2. Conduct whatever research is needed to create a profile of the person or event. Decide how the key facts might be illustrated on a shield. Keep notes to include in your factual summary for the back of the shield.

3. Design and create a group shield and supporting data sheet to display on the back.

4. Present your shield to the class and explain how the symbols represent and depict the key background information on the person or event. Shields will be displayed with those of other groups.

ORGANIZING THE GROUP

1. **Group Work/Decision Making** As a group, decide what event or person to represent and assign the additional research needed. Appoint a recorder to collect the information from group members. Assign roles to group members deciding who will design and illustrate the shield and who will compile and write the summary for the back of the shield.

2. **Individual Work** Do research to find out as much as possible about your chosen person or event. Think about how the key facts might be represented graphically on the shield and keep notes or rough sketches of your ideas. Consider how the information might be organized and summarized on the accompanying fact sheet for the back of the shield.

Cooperative Learning Activity 9 (continued)

3. **Group Work/Decision Making** Share your research as a group. Invite comments on, and extensions to, individuals' ideas and information. Together, decide what information to prioritize and incorporate into the design of the shield.

4. **Group Work/Decision Making** Select a basic design for the shield and decide on the media that will be used to create the shield.

5. **Additional Group Work** Divide the group into subteams to create the front and back of the shield. Decide on one or more group members to present the final product to the class.

6. **Group Sharing** Present the shield to the class, explaining how each individual symbol or visual used conveys information about the chosen person or event.

GROUP PROCESS QUESTIONS

- What is the most important thing you learned about the period of the Crusades from this activity?
- What part of the project did you enjoy most?
- What problems did you have working as a group or individually?
- How did you solve the problems?
- How was it helpful to work with others?

Quick CHECK ✔

1. Was the goal of the assignment clear at all times?

_____

_____

2. How was designing a shield different from other types of cooperative projects?

_____

_____

3. Did you have problems working together? If so, how did you solve them?

_____

_____

4. Were you satisfied with your work on this project? Why or why not?

_____

_____

HISTORY SIMULATION ACTIVITY 9

Illumination

The Byzantine Empire's geographic location, close ties to the Christian religion, and varied cultural achievements affected the course of its 1,000–year history. This activity calls for students to work together to understand certain elements of Byzantine society.

Learning Objective To "illuminate" some facts about Byzantine and Slavic civilizations.

Activity Two teams will develop and play a game based on information from this chapter, including the special features and photograph and art captions. Students will first meet as teams, then divide into smaller working groups of two to four within each team to develop questions and answers for five categories: geography, religion, art, people, and history. After recording the questions and answers on color-coded cards, each team will turn the cards in to you. You can then begin the game.

Teacher Preparation Make a copy of the Illumination worksheet for each student. Gather the following supplies: 60 index cards, 5 different-colored marking pens, 5 white letter-sized envelopes, and a one-minute timer.

Activity Guidelines

1. Explain to students that they are to develop a game based on material from this chapter to help them learn and recall key facts about the Byzantines and Slavs.

2. Organize the class into two teams. Then subdivide each team into five groups of two to four, depending on the number of students per team. Give each team 30 index cards and a worksheet for each student.

3. Explain that students are to work together to develop six questions and answers in each of the five categories. (List the categories on the chalkboard.) Each group within a team will choose one of the categories. Have each student write questions and answers on paper, then let each group choose six to record on index cards, putting the question on one side and the answer on the other.

4. Allow half of one class period for game preparation. Have teams turn in the five sets of cards to you when they are completed. Put all cards of one category into an envelope and mark the outside with one of the colored pens to designate the category.

5. Allow another whole or half period to play the game. One team selects a category. The other team reads the ANSWER from a card, sets the one-minute timer, and tries to come up with a question to fit it. Team members may confer. Play passes to the other team if the response is incorrect. Each correct response counts 5 points. Continue until all cards have been used. The team with the highest score wins.

CHAPTER 9

HANDOUT MATERIAL

Illumination—Worksheet

Check the box next to your group's category:

☐ Geography ☐ Religion ☐ Art ☐ People ☐ History

Question/Answer Sheet

1. Q _____

A _____

2. Q _____

A _____

3. Q _____

A _____

4. Q _____

A _____

5. Q _____

A _____

6. Q _____

A _____

Team Score: _____

Name _____ Date _____ Class _____

Emerging Europe and the Byzantine Empire

DIRECTIONS: Look at the events listed on the time line below. Then answer the questions in the space provided.

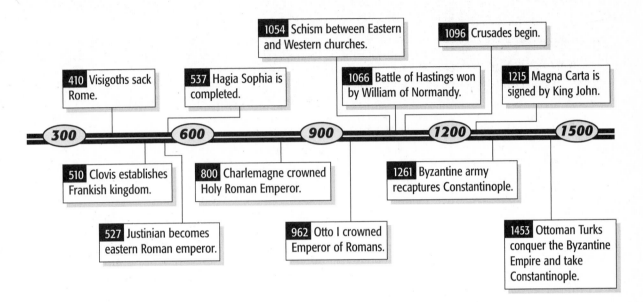

1054 Schism between Eastern and Western churches.

1096 Crusades begin.

410 Visigoths sack Rome.

537 Hagia Sophia is completed.

1066 Battle of Hastings won by William of Normandy.

1215 Magna Carta is signed by King John.

300   600   900   1200   1500

510 Clovis establishes Frankish kingdom.

800 Charlemagne crowned Holy Roman Emperor.

1261 Byzantine army recaptures Constantinople.

527 Justinian becomes eastern Roman emperor.

962 Otto I crowned Emperor of Romans.

1453 Ottoman Turks conquer the Byzantine Empire and take Constantinople.

1. How many years passed between the beginning of the Crusades and the loss of Constantinople to the Turks?

_____

2. Who began to rule the Holy Roman Empire in the 900s? _____

_____

3. Who began to rule England in the 1000s? _____

4. In the early 1200s, who was forced to sign an agreement with his nobles?

_____

5. How long did the Byzantine empire continue after Constantinople was recaptured?

_____

6. When did the Pope lose control over the Eastern church? _____

7. How long did it take Justinian to build Hagia Sophia after he became emperor?

_____

8. Which Germanic people moved into the Western Roman Empire?

_____

Parliament: Medieval England and Today's United Kingdom

THEN The Magna Carta was a document that required that the monarch consult his or her subjects before imposing taxes on them. This rule was an important step in the development of the British Parliament. The monarch met with prominent citizens about taxation, funding for military affairs, and other legal issues that could not be settled in court. This helped to create the framework and precedents necessary for a governing body such as the Parliament.

The first Parliament was made up of the House of Lords and the House of Commons. The House of Lords consisted of all of the nobles and church leaders (the prominent citizens) in England. Their seats were hereditary or, in the case of the church leaders, passed on to their successors. Two knights from each county and two people from every town were either appointed or elected to the House of Commons.

As time went on, members of Parliament began to submit possible laws, or bills, for the king's approval. Eventually, both houses of Parliament, as well as the king, had to agree on a bill before it could become law. By the time of the Tudor kings, most laws would originate in Parliament, where sessions were lasting longer, and its members were developing more sophisticated political skills.

In spite of these advances, Parliament mainly served the privileged classes. The House of Lords played a more active legislative role than did the House of Commons.

NOW Today the prime minister, rather than the monarch, is the leader of the United Kingdom. He or she selects the cabinet of ministers, or department heads, who set domestic and foreign policy. Most of these ministers are members of Parliament.

The prime minister's chief function is legislative. If the majority party does not pass a law submitted by the prime minister, citizens of the United Kingdom must elect different members of Parliament, who then choose a new prime minister.

The duties of the monarch are chiefly symbolic and ceremonial. The king or queen formally "appoints" the prime minister, who has, in fact, already been elected. The monarch presides at the opening of each new session of Parliament yet exerts no power in parliamentary affairs.

The political party that wins the most seats in the House of Commons during a general election chooses the prime minister. Therefore, the House of Commons is the dominant house in Parliament, unlike earlier times. Members of the House of Commons are also responsible for monitoring the work of the cabinet ministers.

Both houses in Parliament take part in making laws, and both debate the issues of the day. However, the power of the House of Lords has greatly diminished. The 1999 House of Lords Act began the process of reducing the number of hereditary peers in that House.

As in the Middle Ages, the United Kingdom's government is centralized. There are no local or state legislatures. Yet today, it is the House of Commons that determines the laws of the land, not the monarch and his or her lords.

CRITICAL THINKING

Directions: Answer the following questions on a separate sheet of paper.
1. **Drawing conclusions:** Why did giving English citizens a voice in making taxes help the development of Parliament?
2. **Making comparisons:** What functions make it possible for the House of Commons to play a greater role in government than the House of Lords?

3. **Synthesizing information:** Wealthy townspeople became the new middle class. Speculate on some ways that the burgesses (and the new middle class) might have been able to gain influence over the monarch. Do research in the library and on the Internet to learn about how the new middle class gained power. Write a brief report of your findings.

People in World History Activity 9

Profile 1

Theodora (c. 500–548)

There are two ways of spreading light: to be/The candle or the mirror that reflects it.

From "Vesalius in Zante," *Artemis to Actaeon* (1909) by Edith Wharton

The Byzantine civilization flourished under Emperor Justinian. His legal reforms have influenced Western law ever since. Scholarship, art, and architecture thrived. Impressive public works projects were completed. But Justinian may not deserve sole credit for these triumphs. His wife, Theodora, is considered by many historians to be fundamentally responsible for the success of his reign.

Theodora was probably born on the island of Cyprus. Her father specialized in training bears for circus work. As a young girl, Theodora participated in circus performances, and in her early teens, she became an actress. At that time performers were held in generally low regard. It seemed unlikely that this daughter of an animal trainer would become an empress.

But Theodora was by all accounts exceptionally intelligent, beautiful, and charming. She married Justinian in 523. The law forbade such a marriage between classes. Justinian, however, ignored the law. Theodora would become his principal ally and adviser.

Detail from mosaic of Theodora

As empress, Theodora championed the rights of women. At her behest, Justinian issued laws against husbands beating their wives. Other new laws allowed women to divorce their husbands and to own property. Widows could keep their children, instead of having to surrender them to a male relative. All of these major reforms were the result of Theodora's influence. She was involved in nearly every aspect of Justinian's reign: the opinions of advisers were often accepted or rejected by Justinian based on Theodora's opinion.

Theodora's most famous contribution came in 532, when government officials organized a revolt among the common people. Justinian panicked and was preparing to flee but Theodora persuaded him to stay and fight. He won and did not face a serious challenge to his reign thereafter.

Theodora died of cancer at about the age of 48. Some historians note a lack of direction and intensity in Justinian's rule after the death of his beloved wife.

CHAPTER 9

REVIEWING THE PROFILE

Directions: Answer the following questions on a separate sheet of paper.

1. Describe Theodora's origins.

2. How did Theodora help the women of the Byzantine Empire?

3. **Critical Thinking** **Making Inferences.** Do you think most of Justinian's subjects knew, or approved, of Theodora's influence? Explain your answer.

> ## People in World History Activity 9
>
> ## Profile 2

Vladimir I (c. 956–1015)

Vladimir I, grand duke of Kiev, was the son of Svyatoslav I, duke of Kiev. Svyatoslav sent his son to rule Novgorod in 972. After his father's death, Vladimir found himself in competition with his two brothers to assume their father's title. He defeated both of them, killing one. Vladimir thereby took control of Kiev and united Novgorod with it. Thus, Vladimir began his rule with expansion. Such expansion and clever statecraft became a hallmark of his reign. Vladimir conquered Slavic tribes and waged war against the Lithuanians, the Bulgars, and the Byzantines.

Vladimir made many important decisions in his capacity as a ruler. He promoted the trade that helped the economy. He ordered the building of schools and libraries. He was an effective warrior who expanded Russia's western borders and defended its people against nomads in the east. However, it was one decision for which Vladimir would be most remembered, a decision that fundamentally changed the history of Russia—and the lives of its people—forever.

In 988, Vladimir, a fervent pagan, converted to Christianity. It is said that Vladimir considered several religions, including Islam, Judaism, Roman Catholicism, and Eastern Orthodoxy, before deciding on Eastern Orthodoxy. He dismissed his four wives and soon thereafter married Princess Anna, the sister of the Byzantine Emperor Basil II. Some historians argue that the benefits of the alliance with the powerful Byzantines may have been a factor in Vladimir's decision to convert and marry Anna.

Regardless of his motives for conversion, Vladimir championed Christianity in his realm. Upon his own conversion, he required his subjects to be baptized. In fact, the people of Kiev were ordered to wade, en masse, into the Dnieper River. He ordered the building of churches, the most famous of which is the Cathedral of the Tithes, and he supported religious charity. Vladimir also gave the church strong legal status. Together, these acts formed the foundation of a Christian tradition in Russia that has lasted nearly 1,000 years. Vladimir died in 1015 and, later, was made a saint. The Feast of Saint Vladimir continues to be celebrated every July 15.

REVIEWING THE PROFILE

Directions: Answer the following questions on a separate sheet of paper.

1. Identify Vladimir's religion before his conversion. To what religion did he convert?

2. How did his conversion affect the people in his domain?

3. What factor do some historians think helped motivate Vladimir's conversion?

4. **Critical Thinking** **Expressing Problems Clearly.** Because of his own religious conversion, Vladimir ordered the conversion of thousands of his subjects. Do you think this was fair? Explain your answer.

5. **Critical Thinking** **Analyzing Information.** After doing research, name two differences in the beliefs or practices between the Catholic and Eastern Orthodox churches.

PRIMARY SOURCE READING 9

The Siege and Capture of Acre

European Crusaders took the city of Acre, Palestine, from Saladin's forces during the Third Crusade, also known as the "Crusade of Kings." (Muslim armies recaptured Acre in 1291.) The passage describes how the English king Richard managed to win the siege of Acre despite the fact that his French allies had been defeated by the Muslims.

Guided Reading   *In this selection, read to learn how the Christian siege and capture of the Southwest Asian city of Acre occurred.*

King Richard . . . was anxious to be doing things and he was free especially to attend to the capture of the city [Acre]. He saw to it therefore that the city was attacked by his men so that, perchance, by divine grace the deed might be accomplished. . . . He had a latticework shed (commonly called a "cercleia") made. It was made solid with many joints, and when it had painstakingly been put together, he ordered it to be taken to the trench outside the city walls. When his most experienced balistarii [soldiers who used the crossbow] were in position, he had himself carried out on a silken litter, so that the Saracens [Turks] might be awed by his presence and also so that he could encourage his men for the fight. His balista [crossbow], with which he was experienced, was then put into action and many were killed by the missiles and spears which he fired. His miners also made an underground passage to the tower at which his siege engines were firing. The miners sought out the foundations of the tower and hacked out part of it. They filled up the hole with timbers which they set afire. Then the repeated hits of the stone missiles suddenly knocked the tower to bits.

The King pondered the difficulties of proceeding in this enterprise and the great bellicosity of his opponents. He decided that, since in the business world work makes progress through excellence, he might more readily attract the spirits of the young by posting a reward than by giving orders through the commanders. Who, indeed, is not attracted by the scent of money?

The King ordered the criers to proclaim that anyone who removed a stone from the wall next to the aforesaid tower would receive two pieces of gold from the King. Later he promised three gold pieces and then four, so that however many

stones anyone removed, he received a payment of four gold pieces for each. Then you could see the young men rush forward and the courageous followers swarm to the wall. When the stones were taken out they would go on eagerly, greedy for praise as well as for payment. Even in the midst of the enemy's missiles they worked on bravely at tearing down the wall. Many of them were wounded, however, and were put out of action. Others, in fear of death, stayed away from danger. But some of them manfully pushed the Turks back from the wall and some of these men were protected neither by shields nor weapons. The wall was extremely high and immoderately thick. The men, however, inspired with courage, overcame danger and removed a great many stones from the massive wall. . . .

Saladin concluded that further delay would be dangerous. He therefore agreed to the requests of the besieged men [to allow them to surrender]. He was persuaded to take this course especially by his emirs, satraps, and powerful friends, some of whom were parents, relatives, and friends of the besieged. . . . He also recalled the wives of the besieged men and the sorrows of their families whom they had not seen now for the three years during which the siege had continued. They said, further, that he would only be losing a city, rather than such upright people.

Saladin's princes persuaded him on these and similar scores and, lest their last state be worse than the first, he agreed that they should make peace on the best terms they could get. It was therefore provided and declared that they would agree to the better peace terms. When the messengers [from the military post of the town] announced the decision of Saladin and his coun-

113

PRIMARY SOURCE READING 9

sellors, the besieged men were overjoyed. The principal men among them came out to our Kings. Through an interpreter they offered to give up the city of Acre, free and clear, and to give up the Holy Cross and two hundred of the Christians whom they held captive and to surrender fifty men.

When our people found these terms unacceptable, the Moslims offered two thousand noble Christians and five hundred lesser captives, whom Saladin would seek out throughout his domains. The Turks were to leave the city, each man taking with him nothing except his clothing. They were to leave behind their weapons, food, and everything else. As ransom

for their captives, moreover, they were to give two hundred thousand Saracen talents [currency] to the two Kings. To assure faithful performance of these terms they were to give as hostages the more noble and important Turks who were to be found in the city.

Our Kings conferred with their wiser men and each other over whether they should allow these terms to be granted. The universal decision on the matter was that the offer was to be received and the conditions accepted. Oaths were taken and the agreement was put into writing as security. Then, when the hostages had been handed over, the Turks left the city empty-handed.

INTERPRETING THE READING

Directions *Use information from the reading to answer the following questions. If necessary, use a separate sheet of paper.*

1. How did King Richard first attempt to end the siege of Acre?

_____

2. What was his rationale for paying people gold coins? How did this strategy help end the siege?

_____

_____

3. What were the terms of surrender Saladin and Richard finally agreed on?

_____

_____

Critical Thinking

4. Identifying Alternatives Do you think that Saladin made the right decision in giving up Acre, based on the advice of his advisers that "he would only be losing a city, rather than such an upright people"? What would you have done in his place?

_____

_____

5. Evaluating Information The selection discusses the siege of Acre from the point of view of many figures involved in the battle. Are these figures accurately representative of *all* the men fighting in the siege? Explain your answer.

_____

_____

Reteaching Activity 9

Emerging Europe and the Byzantine Empire

Even though medieval Europe encompassed a large landmass and many people, it was united by interrelated political and religious systems. Often one particular event, or cause, had a number of effects.

DIRECTIONS: Read the chart below to review some of the important events discussed in Chapter 9. Then provide a cause for each set of effects. You may need to review the chapter to find the causes.

Cause	Effects
1.	• Western Europeans ruled by central government • Increase in learning and scholarship • Alliance established between pope and Frankish Empire
2.	• Villages and towns sacked • Western Europe becomes weakly centralized • Local officials and lords gain power
3.	• Monastic movement begins • Papacy gains source of political power
4.	• Lords grant fiefs to vassals • Vassals pay homage to lords
5.	• Anglo-Saxon and Norman cultures merge • Census taken in England
6.	• The English king's power becomes limited • Nobles establish feudal rights • Freemen guaranteed right of trial by jury
7.	• Italian port cities prosper • European armies travel to the Holy Land

★ Enrichment Activity 9

Religious Faith Meets Nationalist Pride

What we call the Eastern Orthodox Church is actually made up of several autonomous, or self-governing, national churches, each of which has its own patriarch. For example, in Russia there is the Russian Orthodox Church, and in Romania, the Romanian Orthodox Church. Throughout history, the establishment of an autonomous national church was a source of nationalist pride as well as political conflict.

Membership in Orthodox Churches

Country	Members of Autonomous Orthodox Church	Total Population
Armenia	3,343,846	3,557,284
Bulgaria	7,458,918	8,775,198
Georgia	4,351,737*	5,725,972
Greece	10,434,560	10,647,511
Macedonia	1,446,867	2,159,503
Romania	16,238,831	23,198,330
Russian Federation	37,477,272	149,909,089
Yugoslavia	7,216,191	11,101,833

* Includes 3,721,881 Georgian Orthodox and 629,856 Russian Orthodox.

DIRECTIONS: Based on the table above, answer the following questions in the space provided.

1. What would be an appropriate title for the table?_____

2. What is the total population of Greece? _____

3. Which two countries are almost entirely Orthodox?_____

4. **a.** What is the total number of Orthodox in Georgia? _____

   b. Among Georgians, about how many times greater is the Georgian Orthodox membership than the Russian Orthodox membership? _____

   c. The Russian Orthodox population makes up about what percentage of Georgia's total population? _____

5. The Russian Orthodox population in the Russian Federation makes up about what percentage of the total population? _____

6. About how many more Romanian Orthodox are there than Greek Orthodox?_____

116

World Art and Music Activity 9

Hagia Sophia

Emperor Justinian wanted Constantinople, the capital of the Byzantine Empire, to have the greatest building in the world. The result was Hagia Sophia (Church of the Holy Wisdom), which remains an architectural master-piece 1,500 years later.

DIRECTIONS: Read the passage below about this Byzantine church, then answer the questions in the space provided.

Hagia Sophia, Istanbul, Turkey

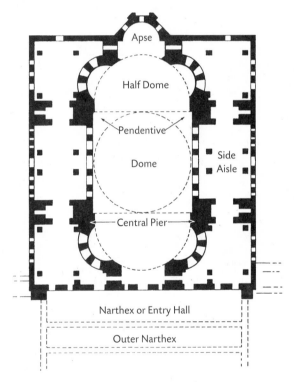

Ground plan of Hagia Sophia

Most buildings are designed by architects. However, Emperor Justinian chose two Greek mathematicians to design Hagia Sophia. The result-ing church, especially its huge dome, combines Greek balance and proportion with Roman engineer-ing skills.

The church is a vast rectangle, measuring 102 feet (31 meters) by 265 feet (81 meters). In the center is a square area topped by a dome. At the front and back of the square are half circles topped by half domes. Along the other sides are aisles, separated from the central nave by pillars. The great central dome has a diameter of 102 feet (31 meters), and the nave rises to a height of 184 feet (56 meters). The dome rests

on four corner supports. Since these "legs" hold up the dome, the walls underneath the arches are not needed for support. Instead, they are made up of columns and windows, which allow light to stream into the church's interior. According to a contempo-rary observer, the dome seems to float "like the radi-ant heavens."

The church's interior decoration had to be large and brightly colored so worshipers could see it from many feet away. The entire interior is therefore cov-ered in colored marble and glowing golden mosaics.

(continued)

World Art and Music Activity 9

The mosaics illustrate stories from the Old Testament and from local history. One of the most famous mosaics is *The Virgin and Child with the Emperors Justinian and Constantine*. On the left side of the Virgin is Justinian, carrying a small church. On the right is Constantine, holding a small city. This symbolically shows that the Byzantine church and state are both in service to heaven.

Reviewing the Selection

1. Describe the form of Hagia Sophia.

_____

_____

_____

_____

2. What was innovative about the dome?

_____

_____

_____

Critical Thinking

3. Making Inferences Worshipers of the time had never been in such a large building. What elements of Hagia Sophia do you think made them feel welcome and comfortable?

_____

_____

_____

_____

4. Predicting Consequences Imagine that the mathematicians hired by Emperor Justinian had been unable to design a system of arches to hold up Hagia Sophia's huge dome. How do you think the design of the church would have been affected?

_____

_____

_____

_____

_____

Glencoe

WORLD
HISTORY

Chapter 9

Section Resources

SECTIONS

Guided Reading Activity 9-1

Transforming the Roman World

DIRECTIONS: Answer the following questions as you read the section.

1. What replaced the Western Roman Empire by 500?

   _____

2. Who were the Anglo-Saxons?

   _____

   _____

3. Which of the German states on the European continent proved long lasting?

   _____

4. What political advantage did Clovis gain when he converted to Christianity?

   _____

5. Describe the crucial social bond among the Germanic peoples.

   _____

   _____

6. What was wergild?

   _____

   _____

7. Explain the importance of a man known as the pope.

   _____

   _____

8. In what endeavor was Pope Gregory I especially active?

   _____

9. What good works did the Christian monks in the new European civilization perform?

   _____

   _____

10. What did the coronation of Charlemagne symbolize?

    _____

    _____

11. Why do we have manuscripts of ancient Roman literary works today?

    _____

    _____

Guided Reading Activity 9-2

Feudalism

DIRECTIONS: As you are reading the section, decide if a statement is true or false. Write **T** if the statement is true or **F** if the statement is false. For all false statements write a corrected statement.

_____ 1. In the ninth and tenth centuries, Western Europe was beset by a wave of invasions from the Muslims and the Magyars.

_____

_____ 2. The most far-reaching attacks of the time came from the Southmen, also known as the Turks.

_____

_____ 3. The Frankish policy of settling the Vikings and converting them to Islam was a deliberate one.

_____

_____ 4. By the eighth century, a man who served a lord in a military capacity was known as a vassal.

_____

_____ 5. For almost five hundred years, men in heavily armored chariots dominated warfare in Europe.

_____

_____ 6. Land was the most important gift a lord could give to a vassal.

_____

_____ 7. In feudal society, loyalty to one's lord was the chief virtue.

_____

_____ 8. In the Middle Ages, men whose chief concern was farming dominated European society.

_____

_____ 9. Social divisions existed between lords and knights based on the extremes of wealth and landholdings.

_____

_____ 10. Chivalry was a code of ethics by which knights were expected to defend the Church and defenseless people, and to treat captives as honored guests.

_____

Guided Reading Activity 9-3

The Growth of European Kingdoms

DIRECTIONS: Fill in the blanks below as you read Section 3.

On October 14, 1066, an army of knights under William of
(1) _____ landed on the coast of England and defeated King Harold
and his foot soldiers at **(2)** _____. William was then crowned king of
(3) _____. The marriage of the **(4)** _____ with the
(5) _____ nobility gradually merged Anglo-Saxon and French into a
new English culture.

The power of the English **(6)** _____ was enlarged during the
reign of Henry II. By King Henry's challenge, four knights went to
(7) _____ and murdered the archbishop **(8)** _____,
who was questioning the king's authority.

At **(9)** _____ in 1215, King John was forced to put his seal on a
document of rights called the **(10)** _____, or the Great Charter. The
Magna Carta was used in later years to strengthen the idea that a monarch's power
was limited, not **(11)** _____. In the thirteenth century, the English
(12) _____ also emerged.

In return for protecting the pope, Otto I was crowned emperor of the
(13) _____ in 962. German king Frederick I considered Italy the center of a "holy empire," as he called it—hence the name **(14)** _____.

The western Slavs eventually formed the Polish and **(15)** _____
kingdoms. The Poles, Czechs, and Hungarians all accepted western
(16) _____ and became part of the Roman Catholic Church and its
Latin culture. Eastern Slavic peoples in the territory of present-day Ukraine and
Russia were eventually dominated by **(17)** _____ rulers called the
Rus. In the thirteenth century, the **(18)** _____ exploded upon the
scene and conquered Russia.

Guided Reading Activity 9-4

The Byzantine Empire and the Crusades

DIRECTIONS: Fill in the blanks below as you read Section 4.

I. Justinian became _____ of the Eastern Roman Empire in 527.

   A. Justinian's most important contribution was his _____ of Roman law.

   B. This simplified code was *The Body of Civil Law*, the basis of

    _____ law.

II. The most serious challenge to the Eastern Roman Empire was the rise of

   _____.

   A. Islamic forces defeated an army of the Eastern Empire at _____ in 636.

   B. By the beginning of the eighth century, the Eastern Empire was much

    _____.

     1. Historians call this smaller empire the _____ Empire.

     2. The _____ church of this Empire was known as the

     _____.

III. The Empire recovered and expanded under emperors known as the

   _____.

   A. The Byzantine Empire was troubled by a growing _____ in its church.

   B. In 1054, Pope Leo IX and the patriarch Michael Cerularius of the Byzantine Church

    formally _____ each other.

IV. From the eleventh to the thirteenth centuries, European Christians conducted military

   expeditions known as the _____.

   A. Warriors of _____ Europe formed the first crusading armies.

   B. In 1187, _____ fell to Muslim forces under Saladin.

   C. Richard the Lionhearted negotiated a settlement whereby Christian

    _____ had free access to Jerusalem.

   D. The first widespread _____ on the Jews began in the context of the

   Crusades.

WORLD HISTORY

Chapter 10 Resources
Europe in the Middle Ages, 1000–1500

CHAPTER 10

Vocabulary Activity 10

Europe in the Middle Ages, 1000–1500

DIRECTIONS: Fill in the terms across and down on the puzzle that match each numbered definition.

Across

1. direct royal taxation on land or property
8. document guaranteeing the rights of townspeople
9. paid apprentice
10. learning that emphasized reason and faith
12. object of religious veneration; a piece of the body or personal item of a saint
13. qualified artisan who could join guild

Down

2. Christian rite
3. unpaid employee learning a trade
4. economic system that replaced barter (two words)
5. language of everyday speech
6. a traveling poet-musician
7. landed estate run by lord
11. to forbid

Skills Reinforcement Activity 10

Analyzing Historical Maps

Historical maps show political, social, and cultural changes over time. To read a historical map: (1) read the title of the map; (2) read the map's key, scale, and labels; (3) identify the order of events to see changes over time; (4) compare historical maps of the same area over different periods of time; and (5) draw conclusions about the causes and effects of the changes you see.

DIRECTIONS: Study the map below. Then answer the questions in the space provided.

1. What historical event is traced in this map?

_____

_____

_____

_____

_____

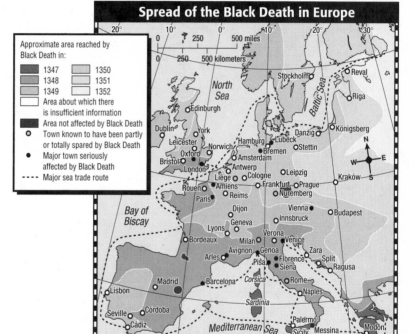

Spread of the Black Death in Europe

2. What time period is represented?

_____

_____

3. What information is shown in the map key?

_____

_____

_____

_____

_____

_____

_____

_____

_____

_____

4. List five cities seriously affected by the plague.

_____

_____

Critical Thinking Skills Activity 10 | Evaluating Information

Evaluating information means analyzing what you read and then drawing conclusions about it. It may also involve recognizing whether the author is biased in any way, even in descriptions.

DIRECTIONS: The following passage from Geoffrey Chaucer's *The Canterbury Tales* describes a medieval monk. After you have read the excerpt, evaluate the information given in the poem.

> There was a monk; a nonpareil was he,
> Who rode, as steward of his monastery,
> The country round; a lover of good sport,
> A manly man, and fit to be an abbot.
> He'd plenty of good horses in his stable,
> And when he went out riding, you could hear
> His bridle jingle in the wind, as clear
> And loud as the monastery chapel-bell.
> Inasmuch as he was keeper of the cell,
> The rule of St. Maurus or St. Benedict
> Being out of date, and also somewhat strict,
> This monk I speak of let old precepts slide,
> And took the modern practice as his guide.
> He didn't give so much as a plucked hen
> For the maxim, 'Hunters are not pious men,'
> Or 'A monk who's heedless of his regimen
> Is much the same as a fish out of water,'
>
> In other words, a monk out of his cloister.
> But that's a text he thought not worth an oyster;
> And I remarked his opinion was sound.
> What use to study, why go round the bend
> With poring over some book in a cloister,
> Or drudging with his hands, to toil and labour
> As Augustine bids? How shall the world go on?
> You can go keep your labour, Augustine!
> So he rode hard—no question about that—
> Kept greyhounds swifter than a bird in flight.
> Hard riding, and the hunting of the hare,
> Were what he loved, and opened his purse for.
> I noticed that his sleeves were edged and trimmed
> With squirrel fur, the finest in the land.
> For fastening his hood beneath his chin,
> He wore an elaborate golden pin,
> Twined with a love-knot at the larger end.

1. What does this monk like more than anything else?

   _____

   _____

2. What does this monk think of the rules of his order?

   _____

   _____

3. What does this monk look like? What is he wearing and what animals does he have?

   _____

   _____

4. Look at Section 4 in your textbook for the reasons why there were calls for reform. Evaluate the description of the monk in terms of the corruption of the Church. Why might a reformer object to the monk's appearance and behavior?

   _____

   _____

   _____

★ HISTORY AND GEOGRAPHY ACTIVITY 10

Gothic Cathedrals

"Whether lifting our eyes to the soaring nave vaults, or peering into the depths of the aisles, the whole atmosphere is one of religious mystery. . . . [One] cannot but experience a little of that unearthly joy so keenly felt by the devotees of our cathedral." What impression do these words by Etienne Houvet, curator of Chartres, give of this French cathedral?

Reflecting the central role of the Church in people's lives during the Middle Ages, cathedrals were built for the glory of God. During the A.D. 1100s, a new system of construction that originated in France signaled a change in architectural style from Romanesque to Gothic. The Gothic style of architecture would allow people to achieve new heights in honoring God.

A fine example of Gothic architecture, Our Lady of Chartres was rebuilt following a fire in A.D. 1194. The new structure, with a vault that reaches 11 stories into the sky, attests to the success of medieval builders in devising new ways to distribute the weight of cathedral walls. Ribbed vaults, pointed arches, and flying buttresses allowed stained-glass windows to fill the interior with light and the walls to stretch to the heavens.

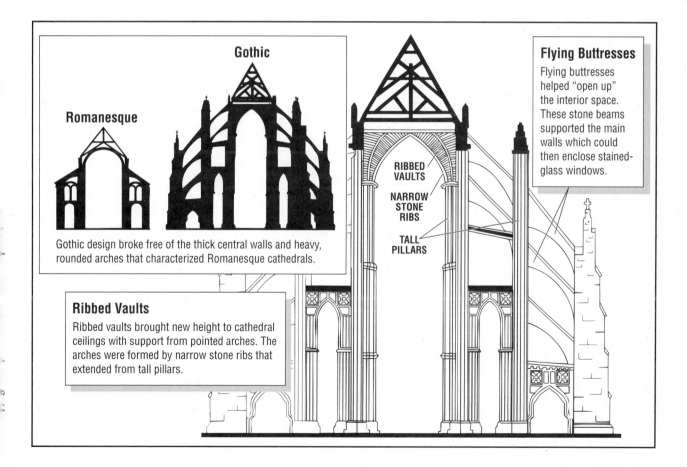

Gothic

Romanesque

Gothic design broke free of the thick central walls and heavy, rounded arches that characterized Romanesque cathedrals.

Flying Buttresses
Flying buttresses helped "open up" the interior space. These stone beams supported the main walls which could then enclose stained-glass windows.

RIBBED VAULTS

NARROW STONE RIBS

TALL PILLARS

Ribbed Vaults
Ribbed vaults brought new height to cathedral ceilings with support from pointed arches. The arches were formed by narrow stone ribs that extended from tall pillars.

HISTORY AND GEOGRAPHY ACTIVITY 10 (continued)

People's ability to modify their surroundings has grown as they have improved their technology. Improvements have been made in tools, transportation, and materials. Gothic cathedrals represent an improvement in design discovered during the Middle Ages. This architectural innovation revolutionized construction and focused the energies of towns and entire regions. Stonemasons, architects, and other skilled workers contributed to this innovation.

APPLYING GEOGRAPHY TO HISTORY

DIRECTIONS: Answer the questions below in the space provided.

1. How can people's use of technology affect their ability to modify their physical environments?

   _____

2. Are there any developing technologies that may affect your physical environment?

   _____

   _____

Critical Thinking

3. **Making Inferences** Medieval cathedrals were centers of religious, educational, and social activities during the Middle Ages. Why do you think it was so important to have such magnificent buildings?

   _____

   _____

4. **Making Comparisons** Compare changes in architectural styles during the Middle Ages with more recent examples of people's modification of their physical environments.

   _____

   _____

Activity

5. To understand how technology can be used to modify physical environments, form three groups to conduct research on physical changes in your community during the past 50 years. The first group will read local newspapers to determine how new technologies were described. The second group will interview members of their families and neighbors to determine the human response to modifications. The third group will contact local officials to discuss how technology has been used to alter the community's physical environment. Each group should present its findings to the class.

Mapping History Activity 10

France in the 1400s

The Hundred Years' War between France and England lasted for 116 years. England had the advantage for the first 92 years, until the time of Joan of Arc. Inspired by Joan of Arc, the French troops began driving the English back to the north of France. When the war ended in 1453, the English had been pushed back to the port of Calais.

DIRECTIONS: The map below shows France in the 1400s. Use the map to answer the questions and complete the activity that follow.

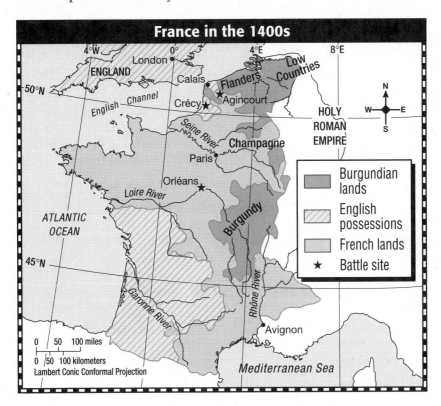

1. Which areas of France were occupied by English forces?

   _____

2. Which areas of France were occupied by French forces?

   _____

3. Name three cities that were strategic battle sites in the Hundred Years' War.

   _____

4. Under Joan of Arc's leadership, the French battled from Orléans to Reims. Reims is approximately 80 miles (120 kilometers) northeast of Paris. Mark Reims on the map. Gradually, the French made their way to Calais. Indicate the French forces' route from Orléans to Calais.

Historical Significance Activity 10

The Beginnings of the Middle Class

In the twelfth to fourteenth centuries, towns began to expand and so did the middle class. The middle class gained its income from buying and selling goods.

Today, in many countries the middle class makes up most of the population. Read this twelfth-century description of medieval Londoners and an early take-out restaurant.

Those engaged in the several kinds of business, sellers of several things, contractors for several kinds of work, are distributed every morning into their several localities and shops. Besides, there is in London on the river bank, among the wines in ships and cellars sold by the vintners, a public cook shop; there eatables are to be found every day, according to the season, dishes of meat, roast, fried and boiled, great and small fish, coarser meats for the poor, more delicate for the rich, of game, fowls, and small birds. If there should come suddenly to any of the citizens friends, weary from a journey and too hungry to like waiting till fresh food is bought and cooked . . . there is all that can be wanted. However great the multitude of soldiers or travellers entering the city, or preparing to go out of it, at any hour of the day or night,—that these may not fast too long and those may not go supperless,—they turn hither, if they please, where every man can refresh himself in his own way. . . .

—From *The Medieval Reader* edited by Norman F. Cantor

DIRECTIONS: Fill in the chart to compare and contrast the description of medieval take-out to take-out today.

Restaurant Take-out: Then and Now		
	Middle Ages	**Today**
Location		
Foods		
Customers		
Reasons for Purchasing		

★ Cooperative Learning Activity 10 ★

A Day in the Life: Europe in the Middle Ages

BACKGROUND

European society during the medieval period was characterized by rigidly stratified classes. The class divisions were derived from the feudal system and were comprised of king and queen, clergy, noble lords and ladies, rural peasants or serfs, and the few merchant or craftsman freemen and their families. By working as a group to create a five-minute play that illustrates life in the Middle Ages, you will learn more about medieval life and society.

GROUP DIRECTIONS

1. As a group, review the roles and classes that made up medieval society in the High Middle Ages from about A.D. 1000 to 1300. Use your textbook Chapters 9 and 10 as a quick reference.

2. Brainstorm ideas for a short dramatic presentation that would illustrate roles and interactions among classes. Be specific about scene, plot, and characters. Describe how the characters would interact and what they would say.

3. Create a script and assign all group members roles in the play. You might want to assign a group leader role to one member to act as director and to another as script or dialogue coach to help individual actors write and deliver their lines and rehearse their roles. Possible roles include the following.

rural peasant	priest
merchant or craftsman	monk
lord/noble	lady/noble
knight	king or queen
bishop	nun

   Your plot and dialogue should showcase the different, yet interdependent, classes that existed in medieval society. The more interaction among the characters and classes that you can build into your drama or comedy, the better your play will be.

4. Present your play to the class. Use props or costume enhancements where possible.

ORGANIZING THE GROUP

1. **Group Work/Decision Making** As a group, appoint a director to oversee the development of the script and the details of the short play. Brainstorm possible scenarios in which medieval roles and characters might interact. Decide on a basic setting and plot for the play. Create a list of characters, with names, to fit into your scene and setting. Assign roles to individuals and let them improvise and spontaneously playact some possible dialogue and plot ideas. The characters might want to use notecards to record their lines. Create a final version of the script from which all the actors will rehearse.

Cooperative Learning Activity 10 (continued)

CHAPTER 10

2. **Individual Work** Practice your lines alone and with a partner. Look for readily available props and costume accessories that would enhance your role-playing.

3. **Group Work** Appoint or vote on a narrator to introduce your play and to set the scene for your audience. Rehearse the play several times to work out the basic staging. Present your group play to the class.

4. **Additional Group Work/Sharing** Invite the members of the audience to comment on the play—did the dialogue and plot illustrate the differences among classes? Let them vote for their favorite character(s). Discuss the likelihood of people from so many different classes interacting in one location, given the strict social divisions of medieval society.

GROUP PROCESS QUESTIONS

- What is the most important thing you learned about medieval society from this activity?
- What part of the project did you enjoy most?
- What problems did you have in planning, creating, rehearsing, and presenting your play?
- How did you solve the problems?
- Did the group members all contribute equally to the effort? Who contributed the most?

Quick **CHECK** ✔

1. Was the goal of the assignment clear at all times?

_____

_____

2. How was producing a play different from other types of projects?

_____

_____

3. Were you satisfied with your work on this project? Why or why not?

_____

_____

_____

_____

HISTORY SIMULATION ACTIVITY 10

Meet the Medievals

This activity reflects the nature of life in medieval western Europe—how strong leadership, security, loyalty, cooperation, and hard work were all necessary for survival.

TEACHER MATERIAL

Learning Objective To introduce students to the people of the Middle Ages; their social standings; and the economic, political, and spiritual interdependency that characterized medieval life.

Activity This activity should be done before students begin reading the chapter. Six students will read aloud from the character descriptions on the worksheet on the next page. The first student will introduce Lord Godwin to the class; the second student will introduce Lady Elizabeth, and so on, until all six characters have been introduced. Then lead a discussion using the questions on the worksheet in order to enhance students' understanding of medieval society and to prepare them for information presented in the chapter.

Teacher Preparation Make one copy of the handout material for each student.

Activity Guidelines

1. Introduce the activity by discussing the concept of interdependence in general. For example, students are dependent on their families, teachers, and friends for certain necessities, such as food and shelter, learning and guidance, or emotional support. People also depend on the students: friends need emotional support from them; employers count on them to do a good job; and parents expect them to work hard in school and abide by the rules. Tell students that medieval society was in many ways similar to their own situation.

2. Explain to students that during this activity they will meet six people of the Middle Ages who come from different social levels and have different needs and responsibilities. Mention that all these people, in one way or another, depended on other people in the social hierarchy.

3. Organize the class into six groups and ask for one volunteer from each group to read an introduction. Write the names *King Jeffrey* and *Lord Godwin* on the chalkboard to begin the diagram that will summarize the interdependent society. As each student introduces a new person, add that person to the diagram with arrows representing his or her connection to those already listed.

4. After all the characters are introduced, have the class discuss the questions in their groups. They must agree on the answers and present a group answer sheet. Each group should select a leader and a recorder and be prepared to discuss their answers with the other groups.

HISTORY SIMULATION ACTIVITY 10

HANDOUT MATERIAL

Meet the Medievals—Worksheet

Lord Godwin of Amsbury

I am Lord Godwin, in the service of King Jeffrey, now the ruler of this region of England. I am the owner of a large estate, granted me by the king in return for my loyalty and my legions of knights. I am sworn to protect my king—a duty I hold as dear as my own life. But I am ambitious and have sent my knights to battle John of Lamprey, lord to King Richard, a possible usurper of the Crown.

Lady Elizabeth

I am wife to Lord Godwin and the mother of his seven children (two of which have died of the plague). I am mistress of the estate, which is no small task, for there are 100 servants, cooks, artisans, and peasants who need my attention. I also keep an herb garden for the medicines my household might need.

Sir Stephen

I am the son of Lord Godwin and will soon become a knight. I have spent several years as a page and squire to a neighboring lord, whom my father trusts. If I can prove myself at tourney, I will earn the right to bear arms for King Jeffrey. Someday he may grant me a fief for my bravery.

Mary, prioress of Saint Agatha

I am the daughter of Lord and Lady Godwin. I would not marry the man my father ordered me to marry, so I have taken refuge in the Convent of Saint Agatha. I will serve God and the good peasants of the nearby village with my skills in medicine that I learned from my mother.

Jack Builder

I am called Jack Builder because I am a mason, a skilled artisan. I have served many an important lord and clergyman. I was an apprentice to the master builder of King Jeffrey's castle, and I was master builder of the cathedral that serves Holy Cross in the Woods. The cathedral is the most important building in town.

Agnes

I am a serf who lives on the estate of Lord Godwin. I work on the estate with my husband and our three children. I pull a plow and sow seeds. In deep winter, I am invited to the great house to help with the needlework and mending. Godwin will always be my lord, unless Richard seizes the throne from King Jeffrey. Then this estate will be granted to John of Lamprey, and he will be our new lord.

1. Which people seem to have the most power? _____

Which seem to have the least power? _____

2. Assumptions we can make about the quality of these people's lives:

_____

3. The political situation here is subject to change. How is this related to the interdependency of various groups of people?

_____

_____

4. At this point, the character we would like to be is _____ because _____

_____

Time Line Activity 10

Europe in the Middle Ages

DIRECTIONS: Medieval Europe in the years A.D. 1000–1500 underwent dramatic conflicts, innovation, and cultural diffusions. Some events of that time are shown on the time line below. Read the time line, then answer the questions that follow.

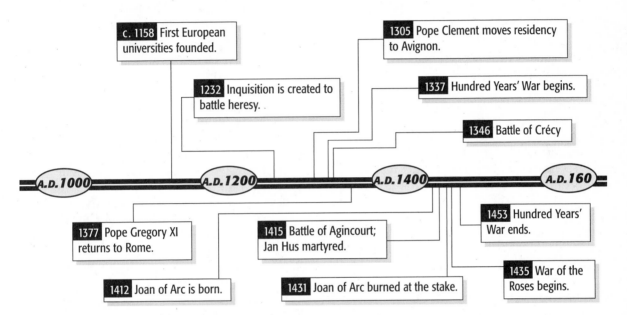

c. 1158 First European universities founded.

1305 Pope Clement moves residency to Avignon.

1232 Inquisition is created to battle heresy.

1337 Hundred Years' War begins.

1346 Battle of Crécy

A.D. **1000**   A.D. **1200**   A.D. **1400**   A.D. **160**

1377 Pope Gregory XI returns to Rome.

1415 Battle of Agincourt; Jan Hus martyred.

1453 Hundred Years' War ends.

1412 Joan of Arc is born.

1431 Joan of Arc burned at the stake.

1435 War of the Roses begins.

1. What important institutions began in the mid-twelfth century?

   _____

2. For how many years was the papal court out of Rome?

   _____

3. During which war was Joan of Arc alive?

   _____

4. How old was Joan of Arc when she died?

   _____

5. What were two important battles of the Hundred Years' War?

   _____

6. During which century did the Church first seek to increase its control over heretics?

   _____

7. What war between the English nobility began in the 1400s?

   _____

Linking Past and Present Activity 10

Old and New Solutions to the Problem of Poverty

THEN In the late Middle Ages, when towns and cities began to develop around local market centers, a variety of charitable institutions began to spring up. Hospitals and almshouses were the most prevalent of these institutions. Originally, hospitals served any person who was in need of either health care or shelter. Almshouses provided food, clothing, and shelter.

Laypeople, as well as religious leaders, founded, supported, and served in these institutions. Some laypeople joined the clergy in charitable organizations called confraternities. Guilds established almshouses for impoverished members and made loans to those temporarily out of work. Guilds also set aside funds to support the widows and orphans of deceased members. City governments ran offices that were dedicated to the relief of poverty. Cities also contributed money to the charitable organizations run by individuals and trade organizations. Wealthy people often willed small annual donations to the poor in their parish.

As urban populations increased, an ever-growing number of poor people further strained the resources of the different support groups. In order to make the distribution of relief to the poor more efficient and effective, city governments began to take on a greater role in distributing aid than did private organizations.

Some civic leaders began to view paupers as potential revolutionaries and/or criminals. To reduce the threat of social unrest, civic leaders designed work programs for beggars and banished them from the city if they refused to work.

NOW Providing for the poor in contemporary society has become a highly centralized function. Although private and religious organizations still play a significant role in fighting poverty, the governments of nations have taken over most of the job. In the United States, individual states make the welfare laws; the federal government provides the funds necessary to enact the different welfare programs.

Most of the Western democracies help their citizens through illness, unemployment, old age, and other periods of financial insecurity. In some countries, the government provides its citizens with medical care. All democratic governments offer a free education through at least secondary school.

Citizens pay taxes to support the benefits they enjoy. Lately, an influx of immigrants to developed nations has placed a heavy burden on these nations' welfare systems. Since many immigrants are unable to secure employment that pays a living wage, they depend upon public assistance. Some people consider this to be unfair, arguing that newcomers to a country should not automatically be supported by that country. Yet others believe that public assistance should be available to all people who live in a country. Most immigrants however, regardless of their income level, still pay their share of taxes.

Lately, government officials have begun to reconsider many welfare policies. Political leaders in the United States have pointed out that issuing welfare checks has created a culture of dependent people. Consequently, they have enacted work programs designed to take people off welfare. In countries with moderate socialist governments—such as Sweden—some citizens have become willing to give up their benefits in exchange for lower taxes.

CRITICAL THINKING

Directions: Answer the following questions on a separate sheet of paper.
1. **Making comparisons:** Compare the sources of money for poor relief in the Middle Ages with those in modern times.
2. **Making inferences:** Why do you think helping the poor is important to the well-being of a community or state?
3. **Synthesizing information:** Why did the leaders of medieval towns take steps against paupers? Do research in the library and on the Internet to discover which legal measures—besides banishment—were taken against petty criminals and vagrants. Write a brief report of your findings and explain how harsh punishment might have contributed to a rise in the crime rate.

> ## People in World History Activity 10
>
> ## Profile 1

Eleanor of Aquitaine (1122–1204)

She was beautiful and just, imposing and modest, humble and elegant . . . who surpassed almost all the queens of the world.

Nuns of Fontevrault in their obituary of Eleanor of Aquitaine

Eleanor of Aquitaine had many impressive titles, including queen—of both France and England. Her turbulent life continues to intrigue people even today, 800 years after her death.

Eleanor was born to a royal family and grew up in an atmosphere of poetry, literature, and music. Her education was not confined to needlework, as often happened with young women. In fact, she learned to read and write Latin and Provençal, the local French dialect. By all accounts, she was beautiful, industrious, and intelligent.

Upon the sudden death of her father, Eleanor became engaged to Louis, the son of the king of France. They were married in 1137, when Eleanor was just 15 and Louis was 16. One week later, Louis's father died, and Eleanor found herself married to the new king of France. Masterful and energetic, Eleanor exercised much control over her husband—and thereby over France. When she accompanied Louis VII on the Second Crusade to Antioch, a disagreement grew between them on strategic policy, which was fueled by his intense jealousy. Their marriage ended in annulment in 1152.

Less than two months later, 29-year-old Eleanor married the 18-year-old grandson of King Henry I of England. Two years later, her husband became King Henry II, and Eleanor was now queen of England. Eleanor was more than 10 years older than her husband, but their marriage was reasonably happy for 15 years, with Eleanor bearing 5 sons and 3 daughters.

Eleanor separated from Henry and moved back to France in 1168, when she discovered Henry had a mistress. Legend states that she ruled at Poitiers over a society of troubadours, knights, and fair ladies who participated in "courts of love." More likely she spent time undermining the loyalty of two of her sons to their father. In 1173, these two sons attempted to seize his French lands, sparking an uprising. Henry squelched the rebellion, captured Eleanor, and put her in prison for her role in the affair. Over time, her confinement was relaxed, and she lived in semifreedom.

Eleanor lived to see her sons Richard and John crowned kings of England. She died at the age of 82 and was buried between her estranged husband Henry II and her son Richard I.

REVIEWING THE PROFILE

Directions: Answer the following questions on a separate sheet of paper.

1. Eleanor of Aquitaine served as queen of which two countries?

2. What in Eleanor's childhood made her one of the most cultured women of her day?

3. **Critical Thinking** **Making Inferences.** Biographies of Eleanor of Aquitaine are popular today, 800 years after her death. Why do you think this is so?

CHAPTER 10

People in World History Activity 10

Profile 2

Isabella I (1451–1504)

You have not converted a man because you have silenced him.

From On Compromise (1874) by Lord John Morley

Isabella was born into the ruling family of Castile, the largest of the four kingdoms in what would become Spain. Her half-brother, Henry IV, was king of Castile. Isabella received a strict Catholic upbringing and was a devout Catholic throughout her life.

At the age of 18, Isabella married Ferdinand, the heir to the throne of Aragon, the other major Spanish kingdom. She became queen of Castile at about the same time her husband Ferdinand became the king of Aragon.

The marriage of the rulers of Spain's two largest kingdoms formed the foundation for the unification of Spain. Isabella and Ferdinand never officially combined their kingdoms, but their major goal was to create a unified Spain with a strong single monarchy. For the next 25 years, they made decisions and followed actions to this end.

In their efforts to unify Spain, Isabella and Ferdinand codified its laws and standardized its currency. Spain's international reputation was enhanced. The king and queen were generous patrons of the arts, and they will always be famous as the rulers who supported Christopher Columbus in his epic voyage. Their reign, however, had disastrous consequences for Spanish Muslims and Jews.

Just two years after ascending the throne, Isabella and Ferdinand started to wage war against the Muslim Moors in southern Spain. It took 11 years, but their forces succeeded in eliminating the Moorish presence. This victory brought Spain almost to within its present borders. The two also waged war on Spain's Jewish population. They ordered Jews to immediately convert to Catholicism or leave the country. In the end, 200,000 Jews were expelled from Spain, and Spain had lost many of its most talented and accomplished citizens. Isabella and Ferdinand, fired by their Catholic fervor, also established the notorious Spanish Inquisition, led by the Roman Catholic priest Tomás de Torquemada. During Torquemada's 15-year reign as inquisitor general, 2,000 people were executed.

Isabella died in 1504 when she was 53 years old. She left behind her 5 children, and a legacy of powerful rule that shapes Spain even today.

REVIEWING THE PROFILE

Directions: Answer the following questions on a separate sheet of paper.

1. What was Isabella and Ferdinand's major goal for Spain?

2. What were Isabella's major achievements as queen?

3. **Critical Thinking** Determining Cause and Effect. How was Isabella's Catholicism reflected in her policies as queen?

4. **Critical Thinking** Determining Relevance. What is the meaning of Lord Morley's statement? How might it relate to the events during Isabella's reign?

PRIMARY SOURCE READING 10

An Italian Writer Describes the Black Death

Giovanni Boccaccio was a fourteenth century Italian writer who wrote the *Decameron*, the story of a group of men and women who survive the Black Death by fleeing their city. Read this excerpt from the introduction of his book to learn more about what it was like during the time of this terrible epidemic.

Guided Reading *In this selection, read to understand some of the effects of an epidemic plague on people in the Middle Ages.*

The symptoms were not the same as in the East, where a gush of blood from the nose was the plain sign of inevitable death; but it began both in men and women with certain swellings in the groin or under the armpit. They grew to the size of a small apple or an egg, more or less, and were vulgarly called tumours. In a short space of time these tumours spread from the two parts named all over the body. Soon after this the symptoms changed and black or purple spots appeared on the arms or thighs or any other part of the body, sometimes a few large ones, sometimes many little ones. These spots were a certain sign of death, just as the original tumour had been and still remained.

No doctor's advice, no medicine could overcome or alleviate this disease, An enormous number of ignorant men and women set up as doctors in addition to those who were trained. Either the disease was such that no treatment was possible or the doctors were so ignorant that they did not know what caused it, and consequently could not administer the proper remedy. In any case very few recovered; most people died within about three days of the appearance of the tumours described above, most of them without any fever or other symptoms.

The violence of this disease was such that the sick communicated it to the healthy who came near them, just as a fire catches anything dry or oily near it. And it even went further. To speak to or go near the sick brought infection and a common death to the living; and to touch the clothes or anything else the sick had touched or worn gave the disease to the person touching.

...Such fear and fanciful notions took possession of the living that almost all of them adopted the same cruel policy, which was entirely to avoid the sick and everything belonging to them. By so doing, each one thought he would secure his own safety.

Some thought that moderate living and the avoidance of all superfluity [non-essentials] would preserve them from the epidemic. They formed small communities, living entirely separate from everybody else. They shut themselves up in houses where there were no sick, eating the finest food and drinking the best wine very temperately, avoiding all excess, allowing no news or discussion of death and sickness, and passing the time in music and suchlike pleasures. Others thought just the opposite. They thought the sure cure for the plague was to drink and be merry, to go about singing and amusing themselves, satisfying every appetite they could, laughing and jesting at what happened. They put their words into practice, spent day and night going from tavern to tavern, drinking immoderately, or went into other people's houses, doing only those things which pleased them. This they could easily do because everyone felt doomed and had abandoned his property, so that most houses became common property and any stranger who went in made use of them as if he had owned them. And with all this bestial [animal] behaviour, they avoided the sick as much as possible.

In this suffering and misery of our city, the authority of human and divine laws almost disappeared, for, like other men, the ministers and the executors of the laws were all dead or sick or shut up with their families, so that no duties were carried out. Every man was therefore able to do as he pleased.

Many others adopted a course of life midway between the two just described. They did not

PRIMARY SOURCE READING 10

restrict their victuals so much as the former, nor allow themselves to be drunken and dissolute like the latter, but satisfied their appetites moderately. They did not shut themselves up, but went about, carrying flowers or scented herbs or perfumes in their hands, in the belief that it was an excellent thing to comfort the brain with such odours; for the whole air was infected with the smell of dead bodies, of sick persons and medicines.

Others again held a still more cruel opinion, which they thought would keep them safe. They said that the only medicine against the plague-stricken was to go right away from them. Men and women, convinced of this and caring about nothing but themselves, abandoned their own city, their own houses, their dwellings, their relatives, their property, and went abroad or at least to the country round Florence, as if God's wrath in punishing men's wickedness with this plague would not follow them but strike only those who remained within the walls of the city, or as if they thought nobody in the city would remain alive and that its last hour had come.

INTERPRETING THE READING

Directions *Use information from the reading to answer the following questions. If necessary, use a separate sheet of paper.*

1. Who was Giovanni Boccaccio?

_____

2. Why do you think the author wrote this introduction to his story?

_____

3. Describe what life was like life during the time of the Black Death according to Boccaccio.

_____

Critical Thinking

4. **Compare and Contrast** Based on the author's descriptions, what were the varying reactions of people to the epidemic?

_____

_____

Reteaching Activity **10**

Europe in the Middle Ages

In the years 1000 to 1500, medieval Europe went through major changes and upheavals that affected all segments of society.

DIRECTIONS: The diagram below shows the five main aspects of medieval Europe. Complete the diagram by listing examples of the most important events, people, countries, and dates under the appropriate heading. A few entries have been done for you.

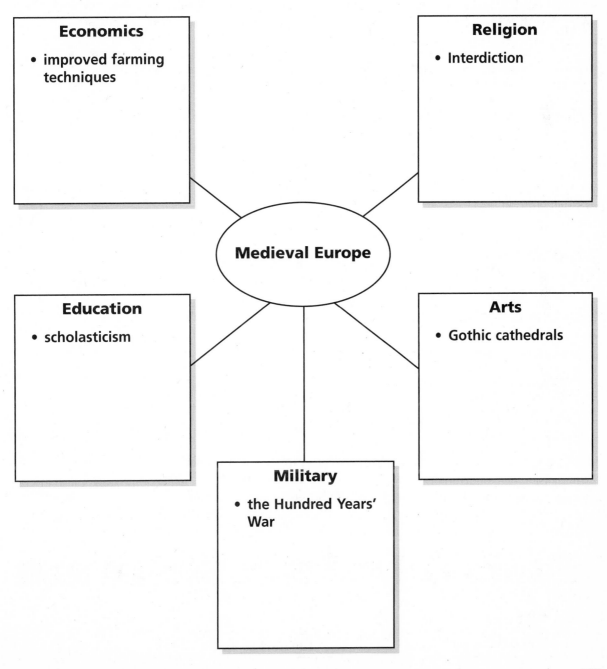

Economics

- improved farming techniques

Religion

- Interdiction

Medieval Europe

Education

- scholasticism

Arts

- Gothic cathedrals

Military

- the Hundred Years' War

CHAPTER 10

★ Enrichment Activity 10

The Noble Household

Chapter 10 describes the lives of the feudal lords and vassals and the living and working conditions of the peasants. One of the important roles at this time was the management of the household, a task often performed by a noblewoman. The description below gives an account of what that task could involve.

A feudal household could be quite large. Important nobles could have a household of as many as 200 people. This meant a lot of management. Some of the work had to be delegated to various people, such as those in charge of the preparation and serving of food and wine or the manufacture and maintenance of clothing and linens. These people, in turn, made sure that the work was done. In addition, enormous quantities of food had to be gathered and purchased. Guests had to be entertained by musicians and performers. Horses and livestock had to be overseen, and farm work carried out and supervised. Children needed to be cared for and educated. Rooms had to be cleaned and warmed. Often, a chapel operated as a church and was attended at least once a day. Letters to lords and vassals had to be written. Rents had to be collected.

DIRECTIONS: Complete the activities below.

1. Imagine that you are the noblewoman of a castle with a household of 50 people. Use the information above and from the textbook to imagine the tasks you have to complete in one day. Fill in the tasks on the following roster.

   4:30 A.M. Daybreak and church

   5:00 A.M. _____

   7:00 A.M. _____

   9:00 A.M. _____

   11:00 A.M. _____

   1:00 P.M. _____

   3:00 P.M. _____

   4:30 P.M. Sundown and church

   5:00 P.M. _____

   7:00 P.M. Bed

2. Imagine that you must provide dinner for your guests and your immediate household—about 15 people. Make a list of items you may need to collect. Think of all the places you may need to travel on your own estate and elsewhere to acquire these things. Make a note about where to get each item. The list is begun for you. Use an extra sheet of paper to continue your list.

Items for Dinner	
Item	**Location**
4 loaves of bread	mill
small jug of cooking oil	market in town

World Art and Music Activity 10

Troubadours

Sometime during the mid-1000s, poet-musicians called troubadours began to appear in southern France. Most were male members of the nobility. Some wrote songs, some sang, and some both wrote and sang. Occasionally, troubadours accompanied themselves on stringed instruments. Their songs—which were sung in the everyday language of the people—were at first taught orally and memorized. It was not until much later that these songs were written down. What this meant was that a troubadour could easily change the words of a song to suit his circumstances. Amazingly, more than 2,500 songs survive.

DIRECTIONS: Read the passage below about these travelling musicians. Then answer the questions in the space provided.

Bas relief scene of medieval troubadours

Troubadour music was composed by and for the upper classes. Knights possessed vast wealth and leisure time, both of which they liked to display. In addition to giving lavish banquets, they pursued the arts in order to gain a reputation for being cultured. Around this time, upper-class women began to be revered and referred to as "ladies."

The words in a troubadour's song were of foremost importance. The music was simple so that it would not interfere with the poetry. The poems tended to be about courtly and chivalrous love, in which a lady was worshiped from afar with great respect and dignity. The object of the troubadour's affection was depicted as so perfect that she was unobtainable. These were not despondent poems, however–the troubadour was content never to possess his beloved. Often the troubadour would imply that he would be disappointed or disillusioned if she accepted his offers.

(continued)

World Art and Music Activity 10

In addition to the worshipful ballads, there were "rescue" ballads called *pastourelles*. All *pastourelles* told one of two stories. In one version, a knight wooed a shepherdess who, after initial resistance, responded. In another version, she called for help, and her brother or lover came to her rescue, driving the knight away. The *pastourelle* began as a dialogue between the knight and the shepherdess. Soon it began to be acted as well as sung. Later other characters were added, along with other songs and dances, to create a musical play.

Troubadour music was very popular. Before long, it spread to England and throughout Europe, as far away as Hungary.

> *Will you love me, O sweetheart,*
> *to whom I have given my love?*
>
> *Night and day I think of you.*
> *Will you love me, O sweetheart?*
>
> *I cannot endure without you,*
> *so much does your great beauty please me.*
>
> *Will you love me, O sweetheart,*
> *to whom I have given my love?*

These two songs represent two different forms popular among troubadours. "Will you love me" is called a *rondeau*, referring to the specific rhyme scheme of its original French lyrics. "King Theobald" is a *jeu-parti*, or a dialogue between two characters, often with differing viewpoints. The authors are unknown, but "King Theobald" is based on the real King Thibault of Navarre in France.

> *King Theobold, Sire, advise me:*
> *For a long time I have dearly loved a lady*
> *With a loyal heart in good faith,*
> *But I dare not tell her my secret,*
> *Because I am so afraid that she will reject*
> *The love which so often ravages me.*
> *Tell me, Sire, what do true lovers do in such cases?*
> *Do they really suffer a pain as intense as they say,*
> *On account of the anguish which comes from love?*
>
> *Young man, I sincerely beg you to be calm;*
> *Do not ask why she hates you,*
> *But be her servant and make sure*
> *She knows what you need in your heart.*
> *For much love is given you to help you serve.*
> *You must proceed by allusion*
> *And knowing looks and signs,*
> *So that she is aware of the suffering and pain*
> *That a true lover feels night and day on her account.*

Reviewing the Selection

1. Who were the troubadours and what did they do?

_____

2. What were troubadour's songs usually about?

_____

Critical Thinking

3. Recognizing Ideologies What set of beliefs about women influenced the songs' "plots"?

_____

4. Determining Relevance Do the lyrics above help you understand the information in the passage? Do they illustrate the points made about the troubadours' love poems? Explain.

_____

Glencoe

WORLD
HISTORY

Chapter 10

Section Resources

SECTIONS

📖 Guided Reading Activity 10-1

Peasants, Trade, and Cities

DIRECTIONS: Answer the following questions as you read Section 1.

1. What happened to the European population in the High Middle Ages?

_____

2. List two reasons for the change in population during this time.

_____

3. What two inventions for the horse made it possible to plow faster?

_____

_____

4. Define the term *manor*.

_____

5. What three ways did serfs pay rent to their lords?

_____

_____

6. Name the three great events celebrated by feasts within the Christian faith.

_____

_____

7. What two features changed the economic foundation of Europe?

_____

_____

8. For what two reasons did merchants build a settlement near a castle?

_____

_____

9. By 1100, what four rights were townspeople getting from local lords?

_____

_____

10. Describe the environment of medieval cities.

_____

_____

11. What three steps did a person complete to become a master in a guild?

_____

_____

Guided Reading Activity 10-2

Christianity and Medieval Civilization

DIRECTIONS: As you are reading the section, decide if a statement is true or false. Write **T** if the statement is true or **F** if the statement is false. For all false statements write a corrected statement.

_____ **1.** Since the fifth century, the popes had been supreme over the affairs of the Church.

_____

_____ **2.** When a church official was given a ring and a staff, these objects symbolized a marriage to God and the responsibility of being a shepherd to his people.

_____

_____ **3.** The struggle between Henry IV and Gregory VII dragged on until a new German king and a new pope reached an agreement in 1122 called the Concordant of Worms.

_____

_____ **4.** An interdict allows priests to give the sacraments to a specific group of people.

_____

_____ **5.** Men, but not women, were allowed to join religious orders after 1050.

_____

_____ **6.** The Cistercian order was founded in 1098 by a group of monks who were unhappy with the lack of discipline at their own Benedictine monastery.

_____

_____ **7.** Most of the learned women of the Middle Ages, especially in Germany, were nuns.

_____

_____ **8.** The experiences of Saint Francis of Assisi led him to become a merchant.

_____

_____ **9.** The Church's desire to have a method of converting more people to Christianity led to the creation of a court called the Inquisition or Holy Office.

_____

_____ **10.** Relics were usually bones of saints or objects connected with the saints.

_____

_____ **11.** Medieval Christians stayed away from holy shrines as dangerous places.

_____

Guided Reading Activity 10-3

The Culture of the High Middle Ages

DIRECTIONS: Fill in the blanks below as you read the section.

I. The _____ as we know it today was a product of the Middle Ages.

   A. The first _____ university appeared in Bologna, Italy.

   B. Teaching at a medieval university was done by a _____ method.

      1. No _____ were given after a series of lectures.

      2. After completing the liberal arts curriculum, a student could go on to study

         _____, _____, or _____.

II. Beginning in the eleventh century, theology was influenced by _____.

   A. Scholasticism harmonized _____ teachings with _____

      philosophers.

   B. Thomas Aquinas's fame came from his attempt to _____ Bible knowl-

      edge with _____ and _____.

III. _____ language is the everyday speech in a particular region.

   A. The most popular vernacular literature of the twelfth century was

      _____ poetry.

   B. Events described in heroic epic poems are _____ and

      _____ contests.

IV. The cathedrals of the eleventh and twelfth century were of the _____

   style.

   A. Stone roofs were heavy so churches required massive _____ and

      _____.

   B. Two innovations made _____ cathedrals possible:

      1. ribbed _____ and pointed _____

      2. the flying _____, a heavy, outside, arched support of stone.

   C. Gothic cathedral walls were filled with magnificent _____ windows.

Guided Reading Activity 10-4

The Late Middle Ages

DIRECTIONS: Fill in the blanks below as you read Section 4.

1. The Black Death was the most devastating _____ disaster in European history.

2. Bubonic plague was spread by black _____ infested with _____ carrying the bacterium.

3. Out of a total European population of 75 million, possibly _____ died.

4. In some towns, _____ were accused of causing the plague by _____ town wells.

5. Because of the plague, trade _____, and some industries _____ greatly.

6. To gain new revenues, King Philip IV of France _____ the clergy.

7. The Great Schism of the Church was caused by the selection of a _____ as pope.

8. Church reformer _____ was convicted of heresy and burned at the stake in 1415.

9. Of all the struggles that took place in this period, the _____ was worst.

10. _____ foot soldiers, not knights, won the main battles of the Hundred Years' War.

11. The English did not have enough _____ to conquer all of France.

12. Joan of Arc came to believe that favorite _____ commanded her to free France.

13. French victory was aided by use of the _____, a new weapon made possible by the invention of _____.

14. The development of a strong French state was advanced by _____.

15. England faced even greater turmoil when the _____ erupted.

16. Ferdinand and Isabella expelled both _____ and _____ from Spain.

17. Almost all of the states of Germany acted _____ of the German ruler.

18. In eastern Europe, rulers found it difficult to _____ their states.

19. Since the thirteenth century, Russia had been dominated by the _____.

SECTION 10-4

151

Glencoe

WORLD HISTORY

Chapter 11 Resources
The Americas, 400–1500

Vocabulary Activity 11

The Americas, 400–1500

DIRECTIONS: Match each term with its definition by writing the correct letter on the blank.

A. maize	**F.** pueblo
B. longhouse	**G.** Mesoamerica
C. clan	**H.** hieroglyph
D. tepee	**I.** tribute
E. adobe	**J.** *quipu*

_____ **1.** large group of related families

_____ **2.** sun-dried brick

_____ **3.** corn

_____ **4.** areas of Mexico and Central America inhabited by the Maya and the Olmec

_____ **5.** payment of money or goods in acknowledgement of submission

_____ **6.** long communal dwelling built of poles and bark

_____ **7.** picture used in writing

_____ **8.** record-keeping device consisting of knotted colored strings

_____ **9.** dwelling consisting of a conical framework of poles covered with skins or bark

_____ **10.** community of multilevel dwellings clustered around a central plaza

11. DIRECTIONS: In the space below write a paragraph using at least five of the terms listed in the box above.

_____

_____

_____

_____

_____

_____

_____

_____

_____

CHAPTER 11

Name _____ Date _____ Class _____

Analyzing Primary and Secondary Sources

Knowing the sources of information found in books and articles is critical to appraising their value as historical sources. Historians need a system to rate the accuracy of the information they collect.

DIRECTIONS: Read the following quotes, and determine which accurately represents the subject being discussed. The criteria to use in making your decisions should be: the type of source, who created it, when and where it was created, its topic, its purpose, and the source's reliability. Then answer the questions below in the space provided.

"The Spaniards had been allowed entry into the city so that they would learn to appreciate the extent of Moctezoma's [Montezuma's] greatness. Instead they seized him as hostage and puppet. As they clustered around him, gazing into his face, touching and prodding him, and then shackled him to teach him fear. His sacred power drained away."

—From *Aztecs: An Interpretation*, by historian Inga Clendinnen, 1991

"When our princes saw the great crowd that had formed there, they ordered that some should set about supplying open-air meals for them all, so that they should not be driven by hunger to disperse again across the heaths. Others were ordered to work on building huts and houses according to plans made by the Inca. Thus our imperial city began to be settled: it was divided into two halves called Hana Cuzco, which as you know, means upper Cuzco, and Hurin Cuzco, or lower Cuzco."

—From *Royal Commentaries of the Incas*, by Garcilaso de la Vega, El Inca, born in Peru in 1539 of Inca and Spanish ancestry. The book was first published in the 1600s and later translated by Harold V. Livermore

"Cicuye is a village of nearly five hundred warriors, who are feared throughout that country. The pueblo is square, situated on a rock, with a large courtyard in the middle containing underground council chambers. The houses are all alike, four stories high. One can go over the top of the whole village without a street to stop him. . . . The people of this village boast that no one has been able to conquer them and they conquer whatever villages they wish."

—From the journal of Pedro de Castañeda, a soldier in the army of Francisco de Coronado, 1560

"In 1531 Francisco Pizarro (ca. 1475–1541) matched Cortes' feat when he conquered the Peruvian empire of the Incas. This conquest vastly extended the territory under Spanish control and became the true source of profit for the crown, when a huge silver mine was discovered in 1545 at Potosí in what is now southern Bolivia. The gold and silver that poured into Spain in the next quarter century helped support Spanish dynastic ambitions in Europe."

—From *Civilizations in the West* by historians Mark Kishlansky, Patrick Geary, and Patricia O'Brien, 1991

1. Which of these sources qualify as primary sources? Secondary sources? Explain your answers.

_____

2. What authority do the authors have?

_____

3. Do you think that materials which have been translated into another language qualify without a doubt as primary sources? Explain your answer.

_____

Critical Thinking Skills Activity 11 | Formulating Questions

Knowing how to ask questions—and what questions to ask—is an important research skill. Researchers of all kinds, whether they are working in history, eco- nomics, biology, or languages, need to formulate questions that will guide their research and lead them to useful informa- tion and theories.

DIRECTIONS: Reread the description of the Mayan civilization in Section 2 of your textbook. Consider the question: "What happened to end the golden age of the Maya more than a thousand years ago?" Then complete the activities below.

1. Formulate three questions that scholars studying the ancient city of Palenque may have asked as they worked.

   a. _____

   _____

   b. _____

   _____

   c. _____

   _____

2. List below three research projects you might undertake for classes or activities with which you are involved. After each project, write one question you have formulated to guide your research.

   a. Project: _____

   Question: _____

   _____

   _____

   b. Project: _____

   Question: _____

   _____

   _____

   c. Project: _____

   Question: _____

   _____

   _____

★ HISTORY AND GEOGRAPHY ACTIVITY 11

What's for Dinner?

As early peoples moved across North America, different groups settled in different regions. People who settled in particular regions developed distinctive cultures. The cultures of northern North Americans reflected their local geography and natural resources.

The diets of early people of the Americas were determined by two factors: locally available food sources and the crops they were able to grow. Along the Pacific coast of North America, people depended mainly on the sea as a source of food. They hunted whales and seals and fished for salmon and bass. They also ate berries and acorns found in the forest, but they did not plant crops. The people who lived in the Southwest hunted small animals, such as birds and rabbits. They also grew kidney beans, squash, and—most importantly—maize.

Maize was first grown about 7,000 years ago near what is now Mexico City. Scientists believe that this grain was intentionally developed by early farmers through a process of careful breeding. From Mesoamerica, maize spread north. By the time the first Europeans arrived in the Americas, this staple crop was grown as far north as southern Canada and as far east as the land along the Mississippi River. Maize was such an important crop that people found ways to improve its cultivation. In the Southwest, people developed irrigation methods to bring water into the dry areas and a system of terraces to control erosion in steeply sloped areas.

The plants in an environment affect the culture of the people who settle there. But the people also affect the environment. Farming brings many changes to an environment. In choosing one plant as a crop, people choose not to grow others. Removing

> *Columbus and the innumerable discoveries that followed his venture across the Atlantic changed many things for the inhabitants of the Old World, but for most people what mattered most was not the new information about the lands, peoples, plants, and animals . . . nor was it the gold and silver treasure. . . . Instead it was a change that historians have often overlooked: the spread of American food crops to Europe, Asia, and Africa.*
>
> —William H. McNeill, "American Food Crops in the Old World"

Maize is not one kind of plant but a group of many varieties. Different varieties produce kernels that are white, yellow, red, brown, and even blue.

HISTORY AND GEOGRAPHY ACTIVITY 11 (continued)

some kinds of plants to grow others can affect the mineral content of the soil. It also affects local animal populations by taking away the preferred food of certain animals.

In addition, farming changes the landforms in an environment. Irrigation channels interrupt once-unbroken fields. Terraces change the slope of a hillside.

APPLYING GEOGRAPHY TO HISTORY

DIRECTIONS: Answer the questions below in the space provided.

1. How does the geography of a region affect what people eat?

   _____

   _____

2. List some ways that people's efforts to get food might affect the geography of where they live.

   _____

   _____

3. Why did farming peoples such as the Anasazi live in villages while nonfarmers such as the Crow, who lived mainly on bison, did not?

   _____

   _____

Critical Thinking

4. **Making Inferences** What other aspects of culture might be affected by a region's geography?

   _____

   _____

5. **Making Inferences** What factors besides geography might affect the culture of a people?

   _____

   _____

Activity

6. Research the Native Americans who lived in your area before 1500. What was their diet like? What were some other ways that they used the geography and natural resources of the area? How did they change the geography?

Name _____ Date _____ Class _____

Mapping History Activity 11

Routes of Trade and Cultural Exchange

When the Europeans reached the Americas, native peoples living there already had their own well-established routes of trade and cultural exchange.

DIRECTIONS: The map below shows a network of exchange centered around the cities of Teotihuacán and Tula. Use the map to answer the questions and complete the activity that follow.

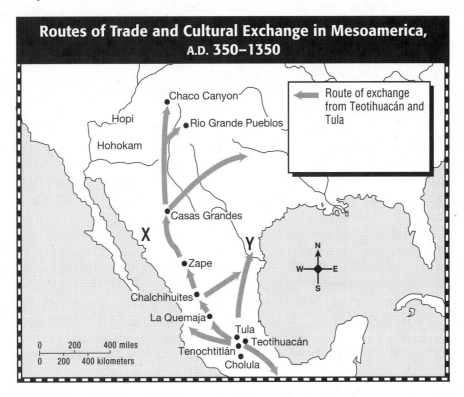

Routes of Trade and Cultural Exchange in Mesoamerica, A.D. 350–1350

1. How far north did the influence of the people of Teotihuacán and Tula extend?

_____

2. Which trade route covers the greater distance, the route from Tula to Zape or the route from Zape to the Rio Grande Pueblos?

_____

3. Using a different type of line or color, draw in the Cholula trade routes as described below. Be sure to add your arrow to the map key.

   The people of Cholula used the following routes of trade and cultural exchange:

   • northwest from Cholula along the west coast to the **X**

   • northeast from Cholula along the east coast to the **Y**

   • from Cholula to Casas Grandes to the Hohokam communities

   • from Cholula to Casas Grandes to the Hopi communities

Historical Significance Activity 11

Earth's Keepers

Many modern Native Americans have become environmental activists in an effort to preserve their ancestral lands that have been so closely linked to their cultures and heritage. The passage below describes some efforts of Native Americans to improve the environment.

In June 1990, on the windswept rodeo grounds of tiny Dilkon, Arizona, on the Navajo Reservation, 300 activists gathered under a revival tent for what would become a watershed event for the Native American environmental movement.

From Wisconsin came Chippewas talking of a proposed copper/zinc mine that threatened their sacred wild-rice lake. Florida Seminoles and New York Mohawks spoke of fishing areas contaminated by industrial mercury. Choctaw and Lakota sat with Hopi and Athabaskans . . . to talk about their environmental battles. . . .

The activists learned that they were facing common problems and even confronting the same companies in their disputes with the mining, timber, and waste industries. And too often, many agreed, they were depending on white lawyers and scientists to fight their well-heeled opponents. What they needed was a clearinghouse for technical information and strategic advice, staffed with Indian experts who could help educate and organize tribal communities to take on big business and big government. From these shared concerns grew the Indigenous Environmental Network. . . .

While the Native Americans may lay claim to being the continent's original environmentalists, tribal movements like IEN are a recent phenomenon—an outgrowth, in part, of the American Indian Movement and militancy about tribal sovereignty and treaty rights, says sociology professor Al Gedicks, author of a book on Native American struggles with multinational corporations. "What good is it to have the right to hunt and fish on your land," Gedicks asks, "if the animals you're hunting are contaminated with toxins?"

The invocation of tribal sovereignty has also become a tool for protecting the environment. . . . One reservation, the Northern Cheyenne, has sought and received Class I designation under the Clean Air Act, which means the tribe has some control over the location and activity of any industry that could affect air quality over its lands. "Tribal sovereignty," suggests IEN's [spokesperson Tom] Goldtooth, "could emerge as the savior of vast ecosystems in the United States."

—From Bruce Selcraig's "Common Ground: Native Americans Join to Stop the Newest of the Indian Wars,"
Sierra, May/June 1994

DIRECTIONS: Answer the following questions on a separate sheet of paper.

1. In what ways did early Native Americans make use of their environment?
2. How are these traditional uses threatened today?
3. Mining and timber industries have looked to reservations as sources of raw materials. Why do you think tribal leaders have considered, and sometimes accepted, these industries?
4. Why might reservation lands be sought after in the twenty-first century?

★ Cooperative Learning Activity 11 ★  ★

Picture Writing in the Americas

BACKGROUND

Before their contact with Europeans, some North American societies recorded stories using picture writings contained in codices (early books). Today, archaeologists use the codices to learn more about life in these cultures. The record found in the codices describes both major events, such as wars and the arrival of Europeans, and everyday life. Emotions are conveyed by facial expressions and by the relative size and position of the people pictured. By working as a group to create stories based on a picture language you devise, you will better understand the importance and appreciate the complexity of pictorial writing systems.

GROUP DIRECTIONS

1. As a group, find and share examples of picture writings. Devise a system of pictures that symbolizes the activities of a modern high school student during a typical weekday. Brainstorm the key activities and ideas that would require their own picture symbol. Be specific about how different symbols could be used. Be creative. But keep in mind the limits of space and memory for your writing system.

2. As a group, devise a picture book of no fewer than 10 pages to relate the events of a typical day in the life of a typical high school student.

3. Individual students should then create personal codices that reflect aspects of their own lives and identities.

ORGANIZING THE GROUP

1. **Decision Making/Group Work** As a group, brainstorm the most important activities that would need to be conveyed in the day of a high school student. Discuss how much detail picture writing symbols can or should contain. Create a list of agreed-upon "standard" symbols, then assign individuals or pairs to produce pages for the book with English translations for each page.

2. **Individual Work** Using the group list of approved symbols, design the pages for the assigned sections of the picture book and write their translations.

3. **Group Work/Decision Making** Share your pages with your group. Invite comments and extensions of the ideas and pages created by individuals. Determine if, when brought together to form the group's book, the individual pages are properly ordered and consistent in their use of symbols and detail. Assemble the pages in the agreed upon order to create the group's picture book.

4. **Group Sharing** Present your book to the class and see if the audience can decipher the meanings of the individual symbols and the overall story.

Cooperative Learning Activity 11 (continued)

5. **Extended Group Work/Sharing** Invite the members of the audience to suggest which symbols in the book were easiest to understand, which were most obscure, and have them draw and suggest alternative ideas for pictures for essential subjects. The group might be interested to examine the advantages and disadvantages of using picture symbols to writing systems; or how pictures might convey differences between verbs and nouns. For example, how could pictures be used to distinguish between the concept of *runner* and the concept *to run*?

GROUP PROCESS QUESTIONS

- What is the most important thing you learned about picture writing systems from this activity?
- What part of the project did you enjoy most?
- What problems did you have?
- How did you solve the problems?
- How was it helpful to work with others?

Quick ✔
ǀCHECK

1. Was the goal of the assignment clear at all times?

_____

_____

_____

_____

2. Did you have problems working together? If so, how did you solve them?

_____

_____

_____

_____

3. Were you satisfied with your work on this project? Why or why not?

_____

_____

_____

_____

HISTORY SIMULATION ACTIVITY *11*

Asking Around

Some of the great civilizations and empires of Mesoamerica and South America lasted hundreds of years. Others were destroyed—prematurely, some might say—with the arrival of European explorers and conquerors.

TEACHER MATERIAL

Learning Objective To practice conducting interviews and recording information about a culture or civilization for purposes of preservation.

Activity In small groups, students will research and record information about a Mesoamerican or South American civilization. Possible topics include government, religion, calendars, foods, art, communications and trade, or rituals and sports.

Teacher Preparation Make one copy of the next page for each student. Bring in supplemental reference books and magazine articles for background information on the Mayan, the Aztec, and the Incan civilizations. If students are to create their volumes in class (see guideline 4), have necessary art supplies such as paper and colored pencils or markers on hand. If students will be using school computers, arrange computer access if necessary.

Activity Guidelines

1. Tell students that much of what we know about the Aztec prior to the Spanish conquest comes from the work of a Franciscan priest, Fray Bernardino de Sahagún, who arrived in the Americas in 1529. He learned Nahuatl, the Aztec language, and, recognizing that the Aztec culture was disappearing, spent decades creating a 12–volume description of every aspect of Aztec culture. His *General*

History of the Things of New Spain is based on interviews with the last of the Aztec who remembered what life was like before the arrival of the Spanish.

2. Organize students into groups of four or six. Assign a civilization (Maya, Aztec, or Inca) and a topic to each group (see Activity). Ask students to decide which members of their group will be interviewers and which will be interviewees speaking as members of the civilization being studied. Distribute a copy of the worksheet to all the interviewers and have students fill in the name of the civilization and the topic.

3. The interviewees in each group will find information about the topic for their civilization, using the reference sources provided. They also will provide a picture—either from a reference source or one they have drawn themselves—of a scene or object that represents an important aspect of their topic. The interviewer will then ask appropriate questions and record the answers on the worksheet.

4. When the interviews are completed, the group will meet to plan a volume of information on the topic they have researched. Using either art supplies or computers, students can create a book that presents and preserves what they have learned.

HISTORY SIMULATION ACTIVITY 11

HANDOUT MATERIAL

Asking Around—Worksheet

Civilization _____

Topic _____

Interviewee _____   Interviewer _____

Ask questions such as the following as you conduct your interview:

What is this called?   Is it used by one person or many?

Where is it found?   How is it used?

Is it hard to find? Are there many of them?   What does it sound like/smell like/taste like/
                                                       feel like?
Who uses it?

**Interviewer's Description or
Sketch of Object:**

**Interviewer's Description or
Sketch of Object:**

**Interviewer's Description or
Sketch of Object:**

**Interviewer's Description or
Sketch of Object:**

Notes on Interview:

_____

_____

_____

_____

_____

Time Line Activity 11

The Americas

DIRECTIONS: Although information about many of the Mesoamerican civilizations remains sketchy, scholars continue to make discoveries about these peoples and the way they viewed the world. Read the time line below and answer the questions that follow.

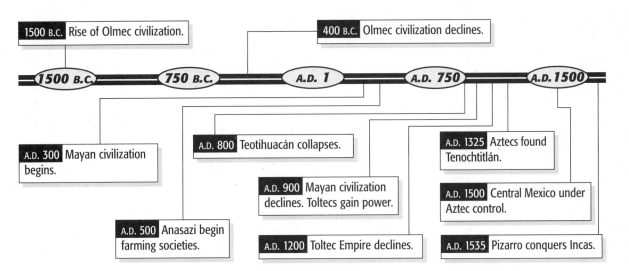

1. How many civilizations are charted on the time line?

   _____

2. Which other civilizations overlap in time with the Maya?

   _____

3. Why do you think these empires existed at the same time without conflict?

   _____

   _____

4. Some scholars have called the Olmec civilization the "mother culture" of Mexico. Explain why.

   _____

   _____

5. If you were an archaeologist and you discovered that a design found on an artifact at a Mayan site matched designs found at a Toltec site, what assumptions could you make and not make about that coincidence?

   _____

   _____

Linking Past and Present Activity 11

Latin American Agriculture: Ancient Wisdom, Modern Mistakes

THEN Mayan civilization developed in regions often inhospitable to farming. In some areas, frequent rainfall created swamps and washed away nutrients. Other areas were dry, hilly, and plagued with infertile soil.

The Maya used the *milpa* system—also known as the slash-and-burn method—to clear land and improve soil quality. Wild growth on a tract of land was cut and then burned. The remaining ash was used as fertilizer.

The Maya often cleared the rain forests to create fields. Newly cleared fields lay fallow from four to seven years. During this time, the growth and decay of wild plants produced rich topsoil.

The Maya developed techniques that helped solve the problems presented by swampy land and irregular terrain. In fields at or above water level, they piled stones on the ground and on the stones. They built terraces in hills to trap the fertile silt that eroded from the slopes. In addition, they dug canals to drain wet areas and irrigate arid ones. The Maya rotated the crops grown on a particular field. Like the Aztec, the Maya probably raised crops on *chinampas* (artificial islands) in marshy lakes.

Advanced farming techniques enabled the Maya to feed their civilization, which at one time consisted of 14 million people. Some scholars believe that despite their best efforts, the Maya eventually found it impossible to keep up with an ever-growing population. According to some, the harsh environment—and the difficulties the Maya faced in farming it—became the primary reason for the eventual decline of the Mayan civilization.

NOW Ranchers and plantation owners throughout Latin America continue to use the slash-and-burn technique to clear land for cultivation. But since these farmers do not let the land lie fallow—as the Maya once did—vast areas have become useless for farming. The owners of large farms also use chemical fertilizers and weed killers on their crops. Eventually, these chemicals poison the surrounding forests and rivers.

As ever-increasing tracts of rain forest are cleared, then misused by farmers and developers, severe ecological changes have begun to take place: the region's pattern of rainfall has become affected, and natural disasters such as droughts and floods have increased.

Latin American plantations and ranches are expensive enterprises. For the most part, their owners do not plant crops that will feed their country's population or put nutrients back into the soil. Instead, they raise cash crops that can be exported for large profits. The economies of some Latin American countries have become dependent on these cash crops. When their value on the world market drops, the countries' economies suffer. In recent years, however, some Latin American countries have begun to diversify their economies.

Various organizations are trying to persuade Latin American leaders that agricultural planners must pay close attention to the story of the Maya. These organizations believe plantation owners should begin to follow the conservation techniques employed long ago by the Maya, as well as develop new ways to successfully farm in a constantly challenging environment.

CRITICAL THINKING

Directions: Answer the following questions on a separate sheet of paper.

1. **Drawing comparisons:** How are Mayan and modern Latin American agricultural techniques similar? How are they different?
2. **Making inferences:** What might be some advantages of a *chinampa*, or floating island?
3. **Synthesizing information:** How do rain forests benefit the world's ecology? Do research in the library and on the Internet to discover why it is important to keep animals and plants in the rain forest from becoming extinct. Write a brief report on your findings.

People in World History Activity 11

Profile 1

Pachacuti (ruled 1438–1471)

The riches that were gathered in the city of Cuzco alone, as capital and court of the Empire, were incredible, for therein were many palaces of dead kings with all the treasure that each amassed in life; and he who began to reign did not touch the estate and wealth of his predecessor but . . . built a new palace and acquired for himself silver and gold and all the rest.

Jesuit Father Bernabé Cobo

A prince once claimed to have seen the lord creator in a dream. When he became the Inca (meaning "king"), he set out to conquer everyone outside the city of Cuzco. He lost many battles to the Chanca peoples, and was even forced to abandon Cuzco. It looked like the end of the Inca dynasty.

His son, Yupanqui, called warriors to defend the Inca from the Chanca army. The Inca captured their enemy's sacred idol, pursued the fleeing Chanca, and destroyed them. Soon, Yupanqui became the new Inca and named himself Pachacuti.

Pachacuti expanded his empire to the sea. He transformed Cuzco into an imperial capital and had a gold-arrayed Sun Temple built to worship Inti, the sun god.

Pachacuti perfected the art of imperial management. He decreed that farmland be used for three purposes: to be cultivated for religious ceremonies in which food and textiles were burned as offerings; to support the government and fill warehouses for distribution in war or famine; and to provide enough food for the populace. He enforced laws that regulated travel, dress, marriage, worship, and proper behavior. He also oversaw the building of the fortress Sacsahuaman. So gigantic is Sacsahuaman that some Spaniards thought it was the work of giants; and some believed the Incas knew an herb for softening and shaping rocks! Actually, some 20,000 men labored 30 years to shape and position the rocks—some weighing more than 100 tons.

When Pachacuti died in 1471, many of his supporters followed him into death by committing suicide. A year of mourning festivals followed in Cuzco. To this day, descendants of the Inca honor Pachacuti in more songs and poems than any other king. Pachacuti created an unprecedented empire. The Inca rule, laws, religion, and language expanded to almost a hundred nations. At its peak, it stretched from what is now central Chile into southern Colombia.

CHAPTER 11

REVIEWING THE PROFILE

Directions: Answer the following questions on a separate sheet of paper.

1. What evidence tells you that Pachacuti was a popular ruler?

2. **Critical Thinking** **Analyzing Information.** How did Pachacuti's three uses of farmland show that he was a great leader?

3. **Critical Thinking** **Drawing Conclusions.** Pachacuti's son, Topa Inca, expanded the Inca Empire as far north as present-day Ecuador. What does the quote by Father Cobo tell you about Topa Inca?

People in World History Activity 11

Profile 2

Itzcoatl (ruled 1424–1440)

In war these people are the cruelest in the world since they do not spare a brother, kinsman or friend, nor will they pardon the life of anyone they capture. Even beautiful women are slaughtered and then eaten.

Spanish conquistador commenting on the fierceness of the Aztec warriors

Itzcoatl was the first and greatest of the Aztec empire builders. He expanded Aztec rule from a single island city-state to an empire of city-states.

This empire builder, however, had surprisingly humble origins. Itzcoatl was born the son of an enslaved girl. One of the unique aspects of Aztec slavery was that it was not hereditary: all children were born free, even the children of the enslaved. There was no shame to being the child of enslaved heritage, and for such a child to become the emperor was not impossible.

Soon after his ascension to emperor, Itzcoatl allied the Aztec city-state Tenochtitlán with the nearby city-state Texcoco. Through the marriage of his sister to a member of Texcoco's royal family, he turned a potential enemy into an ally and began Aztec expansion.

Itzcoatl also began to prepare for war. He seemed determined to resolve the long-standing conflict between Tenochtitlán and the city-state Azcapotzalco. The warriors of

Name glyph for Itzcoatl, whose name translates as "obsidian serpent"

Azcapotzalco would kill Aztec on sight. Itzcoatl persuaded his nephew to go to the city and meet with the king to beg for peace. The king refused, and war was declared. Itzcoatl promised the people of Tenochtitlán victory and rallied them against the enemy. Itzcoatl, true to his word, led them to a bloody victory. His warriors destroyed Azcapotzalco and killed virtually every man, woman, and child. The few survivors were enslaved. Itzcoatl honored his victorious Aztec warriors—many of them his own brothers, cousins, and nephews—with noble titles.

The destruction of Azcapotzalco was the first of many victories for Itzcoatl. Through war, intimidation, and massacre, Itzcoatl led the growth of the Aztec from an island city-state to an empire. As Itzcoatl lay dying, he requested that the king who would take his place build a lavish temple to the gods. He ordered that his image be carved in stone for an everlasting memorial. Itzcoatl's funeral rites lasted for 80 days.

REVIEWING THE PROFILE

Directions: Answer the following questions on a separate sheet of paper.

1. What aspect of Aztec culture made it possible for the son of an enslaved girl to become emperor?

2. **Critical Thinking** Making Comparisons. Compare Itzcoatl's approaches to dealing with the rival city-states of Texcoco and Azcapotzalco.

3. **Critical Thinking** Recognizing Bias. Spanish invaders destroyed the Aztec Empire in the early 1500s. How might this knowledge affect your understanding of the conquistador's comments? How might descendants of Itzcoatl describe the invading conquistadors?

PRIMARY SOURCE READING 11

"Raven's Great Adventure" and "The Origin of Yosemite"

Long before the first Europeans arrived in North America, Native Americans lived throughout the continent. Each group handed down stories to explain how or why something in nature originated. These legends are sometimes based on facts, but they often contain exaggerated details and characters. "Raven's Great Adventure" tells about a bird believed to possess extraordinary powers. "The Origin of Yosemite" tells how the "Ah-wah-nees," the "Deep Grass Valley" people, became known as the Yosemite of America's West.

Guided Reading *In this selection, read to learn how these Native American peoples explain how Raven lost his beak and how the Yosemites got their name.*

Raven's Great Adventure

One day, Raven took the form of a little, bent-over old man to walk through a forest. He wore a long white beard and walked slowly. After a while, Raven felt hungry. As he thought about this, he came to the edge of the forest near a village on the beach. There, many people were fishing for halibut.

In a flash, Raven thought of a scheme. He dived into the sea and swam to the spot where the fishermen dangled their hooks. Raven gobbled their bait, swimming from one hook to another. Each time Raven stole bait, the fishermen felt a tug on their lines. When the lines were pulled in, there was neither fish nor bait.

But Raven worked his trick once too often. When Houskana, an expert fisherman, felt a tug, he jerked his line quickly, hooking something heavy. Raven's jaw had caught on the hook! While Houskana tugged on his line, Raven pulled in the opposite direction. Then Raven grabbed hold of some rocks at the bottom of the sea and called, "O rocks, O please help me!" But the rocks paid no attention.

Because of his great pain, Raven said to his jaw, "Break off, O jaw, for I am too tired." His jaw obeyed, and it broke off.

Houskana pulled in his line immediately. On his hook was a man's jaw with a long white beard! It looked horrible enough to scare anyone. Houskana and the other fishermen were very frightened, because they thought the jaw might belong to some evil spirit. They picked up their feet and ran as fast as they could to the chief's house.

Raven came out of the water and followed the fishermen. Though he was in great pain for lack of his jaw, no one noticed anything wrong because he covered the lower part of his face with his blanket.

The chief and the people examined the jaw that was hanging on the halibut hook. It was handed from one to another, and finally to Raven, who said, "Oh, this is a wonder to behold!" as he threw back his blanket and replaced his jaw.

Raven performed his magic so quickly that no one had time to see what was happening. As soon as Raven's jaw was firmly in place again, he turned himself into a bird and flew out through the smoke hole of the chief's house. Only then did the people begin to realize it was the trickster Raven who had stolen their bait and been hooked on Houskana's fishing line.

On the totem pole, Raven was carved, not as the old man, but as himself without his beak, a reminder of how the old man lost his jaw.

The Origin of Yosemite

Ah-wah-nees were proud of their Chief, a tall and young athletic man. Early one spring morning, he started off with his spears in hand to hunt for trout in the nearby lake known as Sleeping Water.

Imagine his astonishment when he rounded a large boulder and came face to face with an enormous grizzly bear, probably just out of its winter hibernation!

Such an unexpected meeting caused both of them to rear back in stunned surprise. Immediately, however, all of the fighting spirit within each arose. They attacked one another furiously! The Chief realized his fighting power was not equal to the great strength of the grizzly.

"What can I do to help myself?" he wondered.

At that moment, he saw an oak limb within reach and grabbed it for a weapon.

"I must do everything possible to subdue this bear, even if it means my own death," he thought while he fought. "I am determined that future Ah-wah-nee children will always remember the proud and brave blood that flowed in the veins of their ancestors."

He pounded heavy blows, one after another, upon the head of the grizzly bear. In return, the young Chief received innumerable cuts from the bear's teeth and claws. They exchanged blows that could have been death blows to either one, if each had not been determined to survive. The grizzly bear's hunger drove him to attack; the Chief's pride, courage, and great height strengthened his defense.

On and on they fought. Then when the Chief saw the eyes of the bear glaze with a cold stare, he knew his great moment had come. With his club raised overhead, the Chief brought down a whopping smash upon the head of the bear, who then slowly slumped to the ground. The Chief charged in to finish the task, making sure the grizzly bear was dead.

Exhausted, the young Chief withdrew a short way to rest, but kept his eyes upon the grizzly bear in case it revived. After some time,

when he was certain of the bear's death, the Chief stepped forward and skinned the animal.

Later, dragging the bearskin behind him, the Chief returned to his village and proclaimed his victory. Young and old braves gathered to welcome him and to praise his success. The young braves took off, following the trail where the bearskin dragged upon the ground. They found the grizzly bear before any other wild animal had a chance to claim it. Immediately, they set to work and butchered the bear and then carried the parts back to their camp.

In the meantime, the braves prepared a huge fire and sent young runners to the outlying camps, inviting all the people to an evening of feasting.

The victory of their young Chief over the enormous grizzly bear astounded all of the Ah-wah-nees. They cheered and cheered their admiration for their great Chief. They renamed their hero, Chief Yo Semitee, which means "Grizzly Bear."

Following the feast, the entire tribe gathered for a victory dance, attired in all their fine beads and fine feathers. Chief Yo Semitee sat and overlooked the celebration, smoking the peace pipe with his tribal council. More feasting and dancing continued most of the night, as Ah-wah-nees showed their affection for their young and strong Chief.

Yo Semitee's children, and finally all of the tribe, became known as Yo Semitees in honor of their brave Chief.

INTERPRETING THE READING

Directions *Use information from the reading to answer the following questions on a separate sheet of paper.*

1. What powers does Raven have?

2. Why does the young chief in "The Origin of Yosemite" fight so fiercely against the grizzly bear?

3. How do the Ah-wah-nees honor their chief's great victory over the bear?

Critical Thinking

4. **Evaluating Information** How would you describe Raven's character?

5. **Recognizing Ideologies** Why was it important that the chief in "The Origin of Yosemite" subdue the bear on his own without help from other Ah-wah-nees?

Reteaching Activity 11

The Americas

Between 30 and 100 million people belonging to more than 2,000 different groups lived in the Americas before the arrival of European explorers. The way these groups lived was affected by local geography as well as by other factors.

DIRECTIONS: The chart below lists three large areas of the Western Hemisphere. Write the names of the peoples listed in the box below in the appropriate columns of the chart.

• Aztec	• Maya	• Anasazi
• Inca	• Moche	• Plains Indians
• Inuit	• Mound Builders	• Toltec
• Iroquois	• Olmec	

Regions of Western Hemisphere

Northern North America	Mesoamerica	South America

★ Enrichment Activity **11**

The Mayan Belief System

In 1970, a young art teacher named Linda Schele visited Mexico as a tourist. She went to Palenque, planning to spend a couple of hours looking at some Mayan ruins. Instead, she spent her entire vacation studying them. She went back to Mexico again and again, and today she is one of the foremost authorities on the meanings of the glyphs, or icons, of the Mayan writing system.

The Maya conception of time, however was very different from our own. Our old adage, "He who does not know history is doomed to repeat it" might have been expressed by the Maya as "He who does not know history cannot predict his own destiny." The Maya believed in a past which has always returned, in historical symmetries—endless cycles repeating patterns already set into the fabric of time and space. By understanding and manipulating this eternal, cyclic framework of possibility, divine rulers hoped to create a favorable destiny for their people. But while the Maya ahauob [rulers] could know only the immediate results of the events they put into motion, we are gradually reclaiming the full scope of their historical accomplishments from the obscurity of the past.

Our challenge then is to interpret this history, recorded in their words, images, and ruins, in a manner comprehensible to the modern mind yet true to the Maya's perceptions of themselves. . . . History unlocks the humanity of the Maya in a way not possible by any other means, for it reveals not only what they did, but how they thought and felt about the nature of reality.

It is important that we acknowledge this history, because only then will a true picture of the Americas emerge. The American chronicle does not begin with the landing of Columbus or the arrival of the Pilgrims, but with the lives of Maya kings in the second century B.C. We who live in this part of the world inherit a written history two millennia old and as important to us as the history of the ancient Egyptians or the Chinese, a history equal in longevity to that of Europe or Asia.

—From *A Forest of Kings: The Untold Story of the Ancient Maya* by Linda Schele and David Freidel.

DIRECTIONS: Answer the questions below in the space provided.

1. Why did the Maya think it was important to record their history? _____

_____

_____

2. What do Linda Schele and David Freidel hope to accomplish through their study of Mayan ruins? _____

_____

_____

3. What do the authors mean by the "American chronicle" beginning in the second century B.C.?

_____

_____

4. Do you agree or disagree that it is important to understand the history of the Maya? Explain your answer on a separate sheet of paper.

World Art and Music Activity 11

Totem Poles

European explorers in North America were amazed by the wood sculptures carved by Northwest Coast Native Americans. They immediately recognized them as art. There were no professional "artists," although some craftspeople were considered by their peers as more gifted. Anyone could produce art; however, carving usually was done by men, while women specialized in pottery, painting, and textiles. What were these carvings for?

DIRECTIONS: Read the passage below. Then answer the questions in the space provided.

Northwest Coast wood carvings, especially totem poles, differed from group to group and from family to family. Totem poles had a number of functions, ranging from religious to social. They were used to commemorate special events, as memorials to the dead, and as grave markers. Each totem pole identified its group or family through specific historical, mythical, and legendary images. Often, the size of the pole communicated the social status of its possessors—the higher the pole, the higher the status.

Totem poles were carved from cedar trees, an abundant resource of the Northwest Coast. The trunks were cut away or hollowed out on one side. The people, gods, and animals were intricately carved one above the other. Sometimes, a single figure comprised the entire pole. After the carving was completed, the pole would be painted in bright colors.

Craftsworkers used a variety of tools to make their carvings, including axes, hatchets, stone and wooden hammers, knives, and chisels. The blades of these tools were made of a hard stone called nephrite, as well as shell and animal horn. As the European presence increased, blades were made of metal as well. Additionally, sharkskin was used as sandpaper.

The oldest form of totem pole was the house post, which supported the roof beams of individual houses. They usually displayed the occupant's family crest, as well as guardian spirits. Guardian spirits were most often animals. They helped and protected a family and even gave it special gifts, such as success in the hunt or an ability to heal. For example, the house post in the "eagle's nest house" illustrates

Northwest Coast totem pole

the young eagle that saved a girl after an epidemic killed her clan. The bird is painted brown, blue, and red, with a bright yellow beak. Its wing feathers protect the girl's face. Other house posts had bears, sharks, wolves, beavers, thunderbirds, and sea monsters, each of which had some special significance.

Totem poles were also given to the dead. Memorial poles were commissioned by a relative in order to claim the status of the deceased. Mortuary poles held the coffin at the top of the carvings. Other poles were erected to mark graves. One represents the legendary shaman Stone Eagle, who could

(continued)

World Art and Music Activity 11

change himself into other beings. Others show eagles, killer whales, beavers, thunderbirds, and a bear holding a child and protectively licking her head.

A common image is a mother bear and her two cubs. The mother bear is Xpisunt, a woman who lived with bears and had twins who were half human and half bear. Legend has it that Xpisunt's brothers killed her bear husband and rescued her and the twins. The twins helped Xpisunt set bear traps, and as a result, all of her descendants were excellent bear hunters.

The thunderbird also appears on many totem poles. It resembles an eagle and it could swallow whales whole. Lightning comes out of its eyes, and when it flies, its wings make the sound of thunder. These powerful beings sometimes acted as people's guardians and guides. They also could be friendly and kind helpers.

Reviewing the Selection

1. How were totem poles made?

_____

_____

2. Why were totem poles made?

_____

_____

Critical Thinking

3. **Making Inferences** What inferences can you make about Native American attitudes toward animals based on the way animals are used in totem pole carvings?

_____

_____

_____

_____

_____

4. **Analyzing Information** Study the photograph of the totem pole. What do you think its function might have been?

_____

_____

_____

_____

_____

_____

Glencoe

Chapter 11

Section Resources

SECTIONS

📖 Guided Reading Activity 11-1

The Peoples of North America

DIRECTIONS: Answer the following questions as you read Section 1.

1. How far does the land area of the Americas extend from the north to the south?

_____

_____

2. What created the Bering Strait between the Asian and North American continents?

_____

_____

3. When the Inuit moved into North America from Asia, what did they have to learn?

_____

_____

4. What are the Hopewell people of the Ohio River valley best known for?

_____

_____

5. Describe the dwelling places of the Iroquois people.

_____

_____

6. How did the activities of Iroquois men and women differ?

_____

_____

7. The Iroquois settled differences among their people by what means?

_____

_____

8. What was the summer activity of the men of the Plains Indians?

_____

_____

9. List the innovations and skills of the Anasazi people between A.D. 500 and 1200.

_____

_____

_____

10. Describe a pueblo.

_____

_____

SECTION 11-1

Guided Reading Activity 11-2

Early Civilizations in Mesoamerica

DIRECTIONS: As you are reading the section, decide if a statement is true or false. Write **T** if the statement is true or **F** if the statement is false. For all false statements write a corrected statement.

_____ **1.** Mesoamerica is a name we use for areas of Alaska and Canada.

_____

_____ **2.** The Olmec people carved colossal stone heads, probably to represent their gods.

_____

_____ **3.** The Maya built very crude and primitive structures as places of worship.

_____

_____ **4.** Mayan cities were built around a central pyramid topped by a religious shrine.

_____

_____ **5.** Rulers of the Mayan city-states claimed to be descended from the Spanish conquerors that invaded their country.

_____

_____ **6.** The name of the supreme god of the Mayans was Thor, god of Thunder.

_____

_____ **7.** In Central America, the Maya practiced human sacrifice as a way to appease the gods.

_____

_____ **8.** The Maya created a sophisticated writing system based on hieroglyphs, or pictures.

_____

_____ **9.** The Toltec were a peace-loving people who rarely strayed into lands other than their own.

_____

_____ **10.** According to their legends, when the Aztec arrived in the Valley of Mexico, other peoples drove them into a snake-infested region.

_____

_____ **11.** When the Aztec saw the Spanish with a cross on their breastplates, they thought that representatives from the Church in Rome had arrived.

_____

SECTION 11-2

Guided Reading Activity 11-3

Early Civilizations in South America

DIRECTIONS: Fill in the blanks below as you read Section 3.

(1) _____ is believed to be one thousand years older than the ancient cities previously known in the **(2)** _____. The city is located in the **(3)** _____ River valley of Peru. A major urban center arose at **(4)** _____ sometime after **(5)** _____.

The **(6)** _____ lived in a small community in the mountains of **(7)** _____ Peru in the late 1300s. In the 1440s, under the leadership of their ruler **(8)** _____, the Inca launched a campaign of conquest that eventually brought the entire region under their control. The Incan state was built on **(9)** _____, so all young men were required to serve in the **(10)** _____. Because they did not make use of the **(11)** _____, supplies were carried on the back of **(12)** _____. A system of some 24,800 miles (39,903 km) of **(13)** _____ extended from the border of modern-day **(14)** _____ to a point south of modern-day **(15)** _____. Various types of bridges, including some of the finest examples of **(16)** _____ bridges in premodern times, were built over **(17)** _____.

The **(18)** _____ of the capital city of Cuzco were the wonder of early **(19)** _____ visitors. Nothing shows the **(20)** _____ genius of the Inca more than the ruins of the abandoned city of **(21)** _____. The Inca had no writing system but instead kept records using a system of **(22)** _____ called the **(23)** _____.

Like the Aztec, the Inca had no immunities to European **(24)** _____. All too soon, **(25)** _____ was devastating entire villages. Even the Incan **(26)** _____ was a victim. By 1535, **(27)** _____ had established a new capital at **(28)** _____ for a new colony of the Spanish Empire.

Answer Key

CHARTING AND GRAPHING ACTIVITY 2

Mansa Musa: doubled the size of Mali and established a central government; opened and protected trade routes; introduced Islam to Mali; took important pilgrimage to Makkah; established Timbuktu as center of Islamic art and civilization

Sunni Ali: powerful Songhai warrior ruler during the late A.D. 1400s who conquered Timbuktu and Jenne; established Songhai rule over most of West African savanna; controlled gold and salt trade

Harun al-Rashid: ruled from A.D. 786 to 809; developed sophisticated urban civilization based on diversity of empire's peoples; worked to ensure equality among Muslims and non-Muslims; great supporter of the arts

Sui Yangdi: cruel second emperor of the Sui dynasty who completed the Grand Canal using forced labor

Tang Xuanzang: Tang dynasty ruler known for his devotion to a commoner's daughter; unable to prevent corruption and plotting

Kublai Khan: grandson of Genghis Khan; established new Chinese dynasty, the Yuan; his capital, Khanbaliq, later became Beijing

Minamoto Yoritomo: powerful noble who created centralized government under a shogun, a military leader who allowed the emperor to stay on his throne but who wielded the real power.

ECONOMICS AND HISTORY ACTIVITY 2

1. Exchange rates enable people to trade in foreign markets while getting a fair value for their own currency.

2. The Silk Road was a trading route throughout Europe, the Middle East, and Asia.

3. Trading companies were needed to organize and manage the movement of goods over the vast distance covered by the Silk Road. Banking firms were needed to help organize the increased economic activity brought about by an ever-growing international trade.

4. The merchant class was a group of people who earned money through work. Merchants were not peasants or royalty. Their power was earned.

5. Trading economies are based upon people's ability to exchange goods. Education and writing skills ensured that people would be able to monitor and keep records of trading activities that were growing larger and more complex.

6. A goldsmith held people's coins—goldsmiths were in the storage business. Banking involves using other people's money in order to earn a profit.

7. Answers will vary, but students should accurately determine the amount of money the item would cost in foreign currency.

8. Answers will vary. Students' charts or diagrams should accurately show the route taken by the product they have chosen.

WORLD LITERATURE READING 2

1. Possible answers: She is clever, inventive, brave, and intelligent.

2. The jinnee is arrogant.

3. Possible answer: Both stories deal with forgiveness, mercy, and compassion.

4. Possible answers: The demon will kill the merchant; the merchant will find a way to have the demon spare his life.

5. In both stories, characters are sentenced to death even though they have not done anything wrong. Shahrazad is in the same situation.

VOCABULARY ACTIVITY 6

1. angel

2. *Hijrah*

3. bazaar

4. sheikh

Answer Key

5. hajj

6. chronicle

7. caliph

8. *shari'ah*

9. dowry

10. mosque

11. arabesque

12. Islam

13. jihad

14. Quran

15. Sultan

SKILLS REINFORCEMENT ACTIVITY 6

Student answers will vary. Possible solutions might include:

Main Idea: Philosophy, Science, and History

1. Ibn-Rushd, commentary on Aristotle's works

2. Created mathematical discipline of algebra

3. Ibn Sina, medical dictionary stresses contagious nature of diseases

4. Ibn-Khaldun, historian

Main Idea: Literature

1. Quran

2. *Rubaiyat*

3. *The 1001 Nights*

4. Omar Khayyám

Main Idea: Art and Architecture

1. Blend of Arab, Turkish, and Persian traditions

2. Great Mosque of Samarra

3. Mosque at Córdoba, Spain

4. Alhambra palace in Granada, Spain

CRITICAL THINKING SKILLS ACTIVITY 6

Answers will vary. Possible answers:

1. The first speaker states that "women belong to men"; therefore men should be able to arrange a marriage in any way they choose.

2. The second speaker believes that times have changed and that women should no longer be controlled by men.

3. A man might support this ideology because it gives him more power or control over women and whom they will marry. While an arranged marriage does not preclude the possibility of the husband and wife growing to love each other, the loss of romantic love is a possible negative consequence to arranged marriage.

4. Women may be dependent on their fathers or other male relatives for financial support and/or protection. One possible benefit of supporting an ideology asserting women's dependence on men is the promise of security and survival it offers.

5. Ideologies may be handed down from generation to generation through religion or education, among family members, or through the state. Thus it appears that changes in farming techniques, recreation, and education may have little impact on an ideology that is passed along through such fundamental social units.

HISTORY AND GEOGRAPHY ACTIVITY 6

1. It can determine the ways in which people settle, grow crops, use resources, and adapt culturally to their surroundings.

2. Students might consider their own surroundings and describe how people live, noting types of shelter used, foods eaten, and social customs.

3. Family ties ensured protection against harsh conditions and tribal competition.

4. Answers might include a description of social customs.

5. Answers should include a discussion of how oil, wealth, and modernization have affected life in Arab countries generally

and how government efforts to integrate the bedouin have met with disagreement and resistance on all sides.

MAPPING HISTORY ACTIVITY 6

1. approximately 200 miles

2. approximately 600 miles

3. west

4. southeast

5. The path should begin at Madinah, go northwest to the Red Sea, then along the coast of Africa, into Spain and France, ending at Tours.

6. approximately 3,750 miles

HISTORICAL SIGNIFICANCE ACTIVITY 6

1. The design of the house was simple, with small shelters, covered areas, and corridors for the faithful.

2. The relationship between Muhammad's original house of worship and the mosque is directly related: the recess marks the direction of prayer, and the minaret replaces the roof that was used to call people to prayer. The dimensions of the courtyard, although similar to the original, have been increased to allow for more people.

3. Answers may vary. The buildings in which people pray communicate many of the central beliefs of the followers of a religion. In the case of Islam, the structure of the mosque emphasizes the connection of the faithful to Muhammad, the founder of their religion. There is a great deal of attention paid to the proper order and arrangement of things in the mosque, which is consistent with Islam's strict code of proper behavior.

COOPERATIVE LEARNING ACTIVITY 6

Students should complete the activity and answer the Group Process and Quick Check

questions. Have students share their responses with their groups or with the class as a whole.

HISTORY SIMULATION ACTIVITY 6

Students should work collaboratively in groups toward achieving the learning objective of the History Simulation Activity.

TIME LINE ACTIVITY 6

1. Baghdad; Abbasid

2. A.D. 630

3. A.D. 732; Umayyad

4. death of Muhammad

5. A.D. 622

6. A.D. 750

7. A.D. 610

8. Ibn Sina; A.D. 950

9. A.D. 650

10. A.D. 680

LINKING PAST AND PRESENT ACTIVITY 6

1. They adapted their laws to local customs, respected local culture, established order, and promoted prosperity.

2. Modern revivalist Muslims are far less tolerant of other peoples and cultures than were their counterparts in the Muslim Empire. Some of the more radical revivalist groups have launched terrorist attacks on Western countries and Israel. In addition, revivalist Muslims of today disagree with, and on some occasions have attacked, countries or Muslim leaders who exhibit a secular approach to Islam.

3. Students should include the following headings, or main topics, in their outlines: the Crusades, the breakup of the Ottoman Empire after World War I, the British support of the establishment of Israel in Palestine, French colonialism in Algeria,

Answer Key

the support by the United States and other Western countries of secular governments in Muslim countries.

PEOPLE IN WORLD HISTORY ACTIVITY 6, PROFILE 1

1. north to the Black and Caspian Seas and along much of the south shore of the Mediterranean

2. by appointing a committee to determine his successor

3. Answers will vary. Possible answer: Umar may have thought that allowing his captured subjects to keep their faith would make them less likely to rebel against him.

PEOPLE IN WORLD HISTORY ACTIVITY 6, PROFILE 2

1. Khayyam worked primarily in the field of algebra.

2. Khayyam did significant work in algebra, including classifying cubic equations, developing the binomial theorem, and solving algebraic equations using geometry. He was part of a team that created an extremely accurate solar calendar. He wrote poetry that has remained popular since its publication in English in 1859.

3. His calculation of the length of a year is amazing because it is so precise. He carried the number to eleven decimal places, and it is exceptionally accurate.

4. Answers will vary.

PRIMARY SOURCE READING 6

1. He became most angry when someone had dishonored God. He stood so long praying that his ankles swelled; he traveled simply and refused riches.

2. He "hated nothing more than lying."

3. Answers will vary. Possible answer: He was just, unassuming, helpful, unpreten-

tious. Unlike a ruler, he mended his own clothes and shoes and helped with household duties, he did not have servants follow behind him, and he turned down the Angel Gabriel's offer of gold.

RETEACHING ACTIVITY 6

Islamic Beliefs and Practices: hajj; Five Pillars of Islam; *shari'ah*; revelations recorded in Quran

Umayyad Dynasty: A.D. 661–750; founded by Mu'awiyah; Battle of Tours; built powerful state; Sunni/Shiite split

Abbasid Dynasty: A.D. 750–1258; Harun al-Rashid; worked to ensure equality among all Muslims, Arab and non-Arab; urban civilization

Islamic Achievements: House of Wisdom; algebra; Ibn Sina; Ibn-Rushd

ENRICHMENT ACTIVITY 6

Answers will vary. Possible answers:

1. The period of fasting is a time of atonement for sins. By fasting, people make themselves more pleasing to God.

2. During Ramadan, the gates of heaven are open and the gates of hell are closed. The physical body is like the gates of hell: it is "closed" to food; the soul is "open" like the gates of heaven because it is no longer dependent on the body, only on God.

3. The feast of Ramadan places the faithful in the hands of God: every day, people are reminded of their dependence on God for even the most basic necessities of life. Because Muslims believe that God decides the fate of the entire world over the course of a single night, the Night of Determination emphasizes how dependent everyone is on God and his mercy.

4. It may be difficult for many students to realize how difficult it is to fast for an entire month. Be sure that students understand that no food or drink— not even water—is allowed all day. Additionally, because the Islamic calendar

does not correspond to the Julian calendar, Ramadan routinely falls during the summer months when it is most difficult to keep the fast, especially in the hot, dry lands of Southwest Asia.

5. Although it is not easy to keep the fast, it is a time of celebration because people are close to their God; because people are undergoing similar hardships, they can support and encourage each other, rather than become discouraged and possibly break the fast.

WORLD ART AND MUSIC ACTIVITY 6

1. Islamic textiles use patterns and repeating geometric shapes which can be seen in this example.

2. Recreating the human form was forbidden.

3. Answers may vary. Possible answers: valued because, as prayer rugs, they served as personal places of worship; valued for the care and skill that goes into carpet's creation; valued as possessions to be traded or given as gifts

4. Answers may vary. Some students may say that the restrictions prevented artists from creating whatever they wanted. Others may say that the restrictions enabled artists to focus their creativity in specific areas.

GUIDED READING ACTIVITY 6-1

1. The Arabs were a Semitic-speaking people who lived in the Arabian Peninsula.

2. Each tribe was ruled by a sheik who was chosen from one of the leading families by a council of elders.

3. The camel was domesticated in the first millennium B.C.

4. All tribes worshiped a massive black meteorite, the Black Stone, placed in the Kaaba in the city of Makkah.

5. He became troubled by the growing gap between what he saw as the simple honesty and generosity of the Bedouins and the greediness of the rich trading elites in the city.

6. Muslims believe Muhammad received revelations from God through the angel Gabriel.

7. The Quran, the holy book of the religion of Islam.

8. The *Hijrah* was the journey of Muhammad and his followers to Madinah.

9. A belief in monotheism (one god), salvation and eternal life, and the necessity of submitting to the will of the one god.

10. Islam does not believe its founder Muhammad was divine.

11. Belief in Allah and Muhammad as his prophet. Prayer five times a day. Giving alms to the poor. Observation of the holy month of Ramadan. Making a pilgrimage to Makkah.

GUIDED READING ACTIVITY 6-2

1. False. Muhammad had never named a successor and he had no sons.

2. True.

3. False. Their courage was enhanced by the belief that Muslim warriors were assured a place in Paradise if they died in battle.

4. False. He was known for using force only when absolutely necessary.

5. True.

6. False. Arab expansion halted when the Arab forces were defeated at the Battle of Tours in Gaul in 732.

7. True.

8. True.

9. True.

Answer Key

GUIDED READING ACTIVITY 6-3

1. prosperous
2. camel
3. banking
4. coins
5. Baghdad
6. Cairo
7. Damascus
8. palaces
9. mosques
10. fresh
11. Quran
12. slaves
13. widespread
14. spiritual
15. social
16. duties
17. responsibilities
18. a dowry
19. divorce

GUIDED READING ACTIVITY 6-4

1. philosophy; Plato, Aristotle
2. numerical
3. astrolabe
4. historian
5. *Rubaiyat*
6. Samarra; Iraq
7. spiritual, political
8. gallery; boiling oil
9. Alhambra
10. representation

VOCABULARY ACTIVITY 7

1. multicultural
2. matrilineal
3. savannas
4. Swahili
5. plateau
6. diviners
7. bronze
8. caravan
9. oral tradition
10. griots
11. mosque
12. Ghana
13. civilization

SKILLS REINFORCEMENT ACTIVITY 7

1. Ibn Battuta, 1304–1377
2. Humanities, General Research, using call number JFD 87–7680
3. 1986, London
4. 357 pages

CRITICAL THINKING SKILLS ACTIVITY 7

1. F
2. O
3. O
4. F
5. F
6. O
7. O
8. F
9.–10. Headlines will vary. Students should be able to explain why each headline is a fact or an opinion.

Answer Key

HISTORY AND GEOGRAPHY ACTIVITY 7

1. The inhabitants of a place change its character through their changing social, political, and religious activities—work, recreation, government building projects, the construction of religious monuments or buildings. Older cities or towns show evidence of earlier types of human activity. Example: a railroad station building where a railroad no longer runs.

2. fishhooks

3. As the people from Jenne-jeno traded with other West Africans and later with Islamic traders, they learned about other places, ideas, and customs. Borrowing from those other cultures, the people of Jenne-jeno brought new ways of living to the city, such as methods of agriculture, techniques and styles of constructing boats or buildings, or even styles of wearing hair or jewelry.

4. Prior to the construction of the wall, Jenne-jeno may have existed as a small scattering of houses and agricultural buildings. As it grew in size and importance in the area, the town may have felt threatened by outsiders who tried to attack the town's storehouses or wealthy citizens' homes.

5. Possible answer: The people of Jenne-jeno may have believed that the terra-cotta statuettes had religious value—offering safety or hospitality to any who owned or displayed such figures.

6. Students should give evidence of land-use changes such as the construction of new housing developments, new roads, or the abandonment of certain sections of a city or town. Encourage students to explain the human activities that would accompany such land-use changes.

MAPPING HISTORY ACTIVITY 7

1. Ghana, Mali, Songhai

2. Niger River

3. Cairo, Tripoli, Fez

4. Students' maps should show trade routes connecting Timbuktu with Taghaza and Niani. A third route should connect Taghaza with Fez; students could show an arrow indicating the arrival in Fez of goods from Europe. Another route should begin in Timbuktu and follow the Niger River south, then across to Kano, El Fasher, and the Nile, where it leads north to Cairo. Finally, a route should begin in the Middle East and follow the Mediterranean coast to Tripoli. A route from Timbuktu via Ghat should meet it there.

HISTORICAL SIGNIFICANCE ACTIVITY 7

1. Arabs, Persians, India, China, North Africa

2. European Union countries, United States

3. natural and agricultural products

4. finished products and manufactured goods

5. The ancient trading patterns across Africa differ from trade patterns today. In the modern world, most of the African nations' trading partners are the United States or countries in Europe. In the ancient world, Africa traded mostly with Arabs and Persians who brought goods to the continent from India and China. In terms of products, Africa continues to supply natural resources to its trading partners and continues to import manufactured goods. For example, in ancient times, African civilizations imported products such as swords, metalware, silk, and porcelain in exchange for gold, wood, and animal skins. Today, because Africa is less industrialized than other regions of the world, it must sell its resources in order to import manufactured goods, machinery, and transport equipment.

Answer Key

COOPERATIVE LEARNING ACTIVITY 7

Students should complete the activity and answer the Group Process and Quick Check questions. Have students share their responses with their groups or with the class as a whole.

HISTORY SIMULATION ACTIVITY 7

Students should work collaboratively in groups toward achieving the learning objective of the History Simulation Activity.

TIME LINE ACTIVITY 7

1. about 840 years
2. the 700s
3. 87 years
4. A.D. 1307
5. Christianity became the kingdom's official religion.
6. 136 years
7. 900 years
8. 500 B.C.

LINKING PAST AND PRESENT ACTIVITY 7

1. *Ghana* means "war chief." It reflects the militaristic nature of Ghanaian society. This is substantiated by the fact that the people of the Ghanaian Empire conquered nearby territory.

2. As in ancient times, much of Ghana's wealth today comes from exporting gold.

3. Many Ghanaians today feel that they are connected to the past glory of the Ghanaian Empire. Ghanaians are proud of many things: being the first colony in Africa to win its independence, having a strong leader who is concerned for the national well-being, having abundant resources such as gold and cocoa that keep the econ-omy healthy, and having an ever-growing supply of electricity. Students may learn through research that Ghana has beautiful beaches and many

historic buildings, such as forts and castles. Ghanaians have a good education system. Ghanaian musicians originated the "high life" style in African pop music. In spite of modernization, Ghanaians continue to practice many of their traditional customs and, through them, express their African identity.

PEOPLE IN WORLD HISTORY ACTIVITY 7, PROFILE 1

1. Two Christian children, shipwrecked off the coast, were brought to live at the court.

2. Answers will vary, but should mention a transition between the old and new religions and Axum's role as a crossroads of culture.

PEOPLE IN WORLD HISTORY ACTIVITY 7, PROFILE 2

1. maintaining order; increasing trade; supporting Islamic culture; enhancing Mali's stature

2. because it was a time of peace and prosperity

3. He combined a strong central government with flexibility about local customs.

4. Islam influenced Mansa Musa.

5. Questions will vary, but should be based on some of the issues raised in the passage.

PRIMARY SOURCE READING ACTIVITY 7

1. Zeila trades in fish and butter. Mogadishu manufactures material of the same name as the town. Both towns possess sheep and camels. Based on the author's description, Zeila was a large but dirty town, while Mogadishu was a large and pleasant town.

2. Both Zeila and Mogadishu practice Islam. The author calls the people of Zeila heretics, people who dissent from their group's religion, implying they do not

Answer Key

practice faithfully. In contrast, the people of Mogadishu seem to have the author's full approval. The Sultan has built a central mosque and prays daily.

3. Answers will vary. Possible answer: People disapproved of a person buying at below market price because it denies other merchants a chance to sell their goods at the higher price. They disapprove of selling without the buyer's host present because the seller could be attempting to cheat the unwitting buyer. The advantage of this practice is that merchants in Mogadishu keep and gain new customers to trade with because they are seen as fair.

4. The author describes Zeila as dirty, vile, and smelly. However, he describes Mogadishu much more kindly, and is careful to describe how pleasant he found his stay.

RETEACHING ACTIVITY 7

Kush: gold, iron, ebony, ivory, luxury goods, slaves; Rome, Arabia, India

Axum: frankincense, myrrh, slaves, textiles, ivory, metal goods, wine, olive oil; India

Ghana, Mali, Songhai: gold, iron, textiles, salt, ivory, animal products, slaves; Arabia, Egypt

East Africa: salt, copper, iron, animal products; Arabia, Persia, India

ENRICHMENT ACTIVITY 7

1. Answers will vary. Here is a sample speech: Members of this council, what can you be thinking? We cannot just move our village to someplace else. We have lived here for generations. My great-grandfather lived just beyond that hill there. I do not see how moving will help our situation. Instead, I propose that we redistribute the land. The fact that our land yields fewer crops every year can be reversed. We only need allow the land to regenerate itself naturally. We should farm different crops on the land. We can also redirect the flow of the river to bring

necessary water to more distant land. That will give us more free land to farm while we leave our current fields fallow. This is what must be done. Moving is only a temporary escape until we unwisely repeat our mistakes in a new area.

2. Answers will vary. Here is a sample plan: Following the fourth moon, all shall abandon this village for a new and yet unknown land. The easiest way to travel is to follow the course of the river. The river will guide us to our new country. Teams will be drawn up to make boats so that we can easily transport our heavy belongings. Only valuable possessions should be brought. The most necessary are tools to build new housing, and cooking vessels to prepare food. The elderly, infirm, and children should be brought by boat along the river. Since most of the 100 villagers are strong and able, they should walk along the riverside until suitable new land is found. Enough provisions should be brought to feed the children and elderly. Other food will be gathered along the route. Three teams of ten men shall be formed as protection squads. The teams will take shifts guarding the villagers as they move along the route.

3. One reason that many people move is war. War creates hardship that make families want to leave to find a safe country in which to live. They may move temporarily to a new country until the war is over, or they may move permanently. Often, families choose a new country if they know that they have a friend or relative who has already moved there. The United States is one destination for many people. For example, many El Salvadoran refugees came to the United States during their civil war in the mid-1980s. Many Vietnamese refugees came to the United States for the same reason in the 1970s. About 2 million people living in the former Yugoslavia became refugees. Many of them settled in Germany, Sweden, and other European countries.

Answer Key

WORLD ART AND MUSIC ACTIVITY 7

1. drums, rattles, and other percussion instruments; xylophones; bells; lutes; horns; flutes; harps; students may also include snapping fingers, clapping hands, and stomping feet

2. The music of most African countries was not written. Until the advent of sound recordings in the twentieth century, together with easier and faster means of transportation among the continents, musicologists had very little evidence to work with.

3. Because northern Africa experienced more interaction with outsiders, its music adapted by incorporating some of the outsiders' traditions and instruments. Music from southern Africa retained more of its indigenous traditions because this region did not have as much contact with outsiders.

4. Answers will vary. Possible answers: because percussion instruments were easily made from the wood, gourds, and animal skins and bones available to Africans all over the continent, and dance and song were important in religious ceremonies and in communication

5. Percussion is much more central to African music than to Western music. More than simply expressing the rhythmic beat, African percussion is often used as a line of melody.

6. Music plays an important role in African cultures. It is part of everyday life and an important part of spiritual ceremonies.

GUIDED READING ACTIVITY 7-1

1. Asia

2. It is the largest desert on the earth.

3. The hump juts like a massive shoulder into the Atlantic Ocean.

4. The Great Rift Valley, where mountains loom over deep canyons.

5. A mile climate zone stretches across the northern coast and southern tip of Africa. Deserts form another climate zone. A third zone is the rain forest along the equator. A final zone is the savannas, grasslands.

6. The Kushites were still using bronze and stone weapons and were overwhelmed by the iron spears and swords of the Assyrians.

7. It emerged as an independent state that combined Arab and African cultures.

8. King Ezana converted to Christianity, which was first brought to Axum by shipwrecked Syrians.

9. The king made Christianity the official religion of Axum.

10. The entire coastal region of North Africa as far west as the Strait of Gibraltar was under Arab rule.

11. Their relations were relatively peaceful.

12. Axum had become deeply involved in a trade conflict with the Muslim state of Adal.

GUIDED READING ACTIVITY 7-2

1. True.

2. False. The kings of Ghana governed without any laws.

3. False. The kingdom prospered from its possession of both iron and gold.

4. True.

5. True.

6. False. Mansa Musa made this pilgrimage as a devout Muslim.

7. False. These cities gave Songhai control of the trading empire, especially trade in salt and gold.

8. True.

9. True.

Answer Key

10. False. The blocks were stacked without the use of mortar.

GUIDED READING ACTIVITY 7-3

I. gulf
   A. complaints
   B. Merchants, taxes
II. identity, family, lineage
   A. merchants
   B. mother
III. Europeans
   A. ancient
   B. Berbers, farming villages
IV. shared, single
   A. Ashanti
   B. ritual
V. rock paintings
   A. spiritual powers
   B. Nok, sculpture
   C. religious

VOCABULARY ACTIVITY 8

1. scholar-gentry

2. dowry

3. khanates

4. porcelain

5. Samurai

6. shoguns

7. Theravada

8. Mahayana

9. archipelago

10. trading societies

11. Bushido

12. Shinto

13. Zen

SKILLS REINFORCEMENT ACTIVITY 8

1. Answers will vary but may include: Harmony is the glue binding society together; Buddhist laws and codes should be worshiped by all; only a minority of people are smart, most are easily influenced.

2. Answers will vary but may include: Following Confucian and Buddhist beliefs will lead to unlimited progress in human affairs; without a universally accepted moral code, human society will degenerate into petty partisan squabbling.

3. Quotes should be appropriately referenced to the central idea identified by students.

CRITICAL THINKING SKILLS ACTIVITY 8

1. Between May and October.
Sittwe = 828 mm (32.2 inches)/month;
Yangon = 397 mm (15.4 inches)/month;
Saigon = 293 mm (11.4 inches)/month

2. Between March and May for Yangon and Saigon; between April and June for Sittwe. The hot season precedes the monsoon season.

3. Because the monsoons are annual, predictable occurrences, people could track the duration of the monsoons and of the dry seasons with reasonable accuracy. From this information, they could plant their crops before the rains fell and perhaps have time to harvest more than one crop during the monsoon season.

4. If the monsoons are light, the people living in Asia probably have poor crop yields because they get relatively little rainfall during the dry season. Poor crop yields, in turn, can create food shortages and, if severe enough, cause famines and starvation.

HISTORY AND GEOGRAPHY ACTIVITY 8

1. Physical characteristics of a place can include climate, landforms, water forms, vegetation, and animal life.

2. India's monsoon season is characterized by a wind that changes direction twice a year. A summer, or southwest, monsoon

Answer Key

blows from mid-May through September, bringing heavy rains from tropical oceans; the winter, or northeast, monsoon is a reverse wind that begins in October and brings cool, dry, continental air.

3. Food production in some rural areas depends on a single growing season; a delay, therefore, can result in crop failure, higher prices, and inflation. Half of India's electricity is generated by water; a delay in the monsoon can lead to power outages.

4. People in rural and urban areas depend on the timely arrival of monsoon rains for a variety of economic, social, and political reasons. Accurate forecasts could help Indians prepare for the effects of the monsoon season.

5. The monsoon season is a significant physical characteristic of life in India; Indians therefore look forward to seeing monsoon clouds and welcome the arrival of rain. However, many people in the West do not depend on this particular aspect of climatic change and may perceive rain and clouds as symbols of sadness and melancholy.

6. Answers will vary. It may be helpful to organize the class into two teams. Have one team research the climate of different areas in the United States, while the other team researches how these differences in climate affect physical and human environments. When each team has completed its list, have volunteers from both groups make a presentation to the entire class.

MAPPING HISTORY ACTIVITY 8

1. Students should correctly label the major Asian language families on the corresponding areas of their maps.

2. Borobudur: Austronesian; Nara: Altaic

3. Students should infer that the Austronesian language family spread throughout the area because people traveling from island to island in boats most likely spread similar languages among the inhabitants of each island.

4. Mainland Southeast Asia consists of several mountain ranges and river valleys that cut the people off from one another.

HISTORICAL SIGNIFICANCE ACTIVITY 8

Answers may vary. Possible answers:

1. Just as blood must flow through all parts of the body if it is to continue to live, so must wealth—the "blood" of the body politic—flow through all levels of Muslim society. The Quran has explicit laws that ensure that businesses compete with one another fairly and that the wealthy help to support the poor.

2. The Quran has laws about practical issues like inheritance, interest on loans, and profit.

COOPERATIVE LEARNING ACTIVITY 8

Students should complete the activity and answer the Group Process and Quick Check questions. Have students share their responses with their groups or with the class as a whole.

HISTORY SIMULATION ACTIVITY 8

Students should work collaboratively in groups toward achieving the learning objective of the History Simulation Activity.

TIME LINE ACTIVITY 8

1. China and Vietnam

2. in 1192

3. Genghis Khan's grandson, Kublai Khan, overthrew the Song dynasty.

4. 630 years

5. Korea; Yi; A.D. 1392

6. 53 years

Answer Key

LINKING PAST AND PRESENT ACTIVITY 8

1. It makes him or her dependent on someone else and subject to that person's will.

2. Some Chinese women became poets and historians.

3. Students will learn that not all women become mothers, and that in China, women tend to have no more than two children — a choice that is greatly encouraged, some say "pushed" by the Communist government. Keeping this in mind, one can assume that most women would be able to manage their job responsibilities along with a small, rather than large, family. In addition, Chinese people often live in extended families. A female manager could leave her baby with a family member while at work. Also, by the time most Chinese women have worked their way up the career ladder, they are usually past childbearing age.

PEOPLE IN WORLD HISTORY ACTIVITY 8, PROFILE 1

1. In his essays Su Dongpo discusses the Confucian ideal of public service, and Buddhist and Daoist ideas about change and nonattachment.

2. The typical Confucian bureaucrat combined public service and politics with culture and the arts.

3. Su Dongpo was imprisoned and exiled for his political views.

4. Students should pick two qualities from the following list of the qualities of Su Dongpo's poetry: its natural, flowing style, a wide variety of subject matter, strong attention to detail, tenderness, playfulness, and humor.

5. Student answers will vary. Accept relevant and thoughtful answers.

PEOPLE IN WORLD HISTORY ACTIVITY 8, PROFILE 2

1. Kanchi, now known as Kanchipuram

2. defeating the Chalukyas, thus securing Pallava rule; founding new cities; commissioning sculptures and buildings

3. Answers will vary. Students may say it is important because people and civilizations learn from their predecessors' achievements and mistakes.

PRIMARY SOURCE READING ACTIVITY 8

1. He asks the Buddha to teach him how to live the virtuous life (honor the six quarters).

2. The Buddha tells him to avoid the four vices of action, to avoid doing deeds stemming from the four evil motives, and not to squander his wealth by the six methods described.

3. Good men give good advice and genuinely seek to help you; evil men say only what a person wants to hear and encourage people to waste their money and engage in wasteful acts.

4. Answers will vary. Possible answer: Followers might be attracted to the simple, clear guidelines the Buddha suggests, as well as to the values of friendship, thrift, and moderation he advocates.

5. The selection shows the Buddha performing common activities, such as begging for food and engaging in conversation with Singala, the householder's son.

RETEACHING ACTIVITY 8

Rulers: Sui—completed the Grand Canal; Tang—restored the power of China in East Asia; Song—economic prosperity and cultural achievement

Ways of Life: Buddhism—Indian religion brought to China by merchants and missionaries; Daoism—harmony with nature; Neo-Confucianism—shaped society and government

Answer Key

Society: Literature—invention of printing; Social Classes—scholar-gentry, peasants, landowners; Family—girl's parents provide a dowry when she marries; Science and Technology—steel, cotton, fire-lance

ENRICHMENT ACTIVITY 8

1. 11 days (29.5 × 12 = 354, 11 days shorter than a 365-day solar year)

2. 30.4 days (365 ÷ 12 = 30.4)

3. about one day (30.4 − 29.5 = 0.9)

4. Answers may range from 30 to 33. At about one day per month, it would take 30 months to lose about 30 days. In fact, the leap month is added every 30 lunar months.

5. Because of international trade, it would be difficult to make date conversions constantly, so the Chinese decided to convert to the calendar used by their Western trading partners.

WORLD ART AND MUSIC ACTIVITY 8

1. Porcelain is a hard object with a durable, glasslike surface. It is made from kaolin, covered with glaze, and fired in a hot kiln.

2. Tang pottery comes in simple shapes with bright-colored glazes. It includes animals and people to be placed in tombs. It was inexpensive. Song pottery was made for the nobility. It used more elaborate shapes and more colors, including the well known blue and white porcelain.

3. As Chinese ceramics progressed through the Tang, Song, and Yuan dynasties, they became more elaborate. Students should predict that Ming ceramics were even more elaborate.

GUIDED READING ACTIVITY 8-1

1. It managed to unify China once again under the emperor's authority.

2. The new canal linked north and south, making it easier to ship rice.

3. They restored the civil service examination to recruit officials for civilian bureaucracy. They tried to create a more stable economy by giving land to the peasants and breaking up the power of the owners of the large estates.

4. economic prosperity and cultural achievement

5. They formed an alliance with the Mongols.

6. China was a monarchy that employed a relatively large bureaucracy. Government was centered around provinces, districts and villages. Confucian ideals were the cement that held the system together.

7. The Chinese economy grew in size and complexity. Agriculture flourished and manufacturing and trade grew dramatically.

8. The Chinese began to make steel which was used to make swords and sickles. The introduction of cotton made it possible to make new kinds of clothes. Gunpowder was invented and used to make explosives.

9. They exported tea, silk, and porcelain. In return they received exotic woods, precious stones, and various tropical goods.

10. Changan

11. In times of famine, female infants might be killed. Poor families often sold their daughters to wealthy villagers.

GUIDED READING ACTIVITY 8-2

1. True.

2. False. The Mongols brought the entire Eurasian landmass under a single rule, creating the largest land empire in history.

3. False. It may be that only the death of Genghis Kahn kept the Mongols from attacking western Europe.

Answer Key

4. False. The city would later be known by the Chinese name Beijing.

5. True.

6. False. Zhu Yuanzhang was the son of a peasant.

7. True.

8. False. Neo-Confucianists believe that although humans live in the material world, each individual is also linked spiritually with the Supreme Ultimate.

9. False. Chinese poems celebrated the beauty of nature, the changes of the seasons, and the joys of friendship.

10. True.

GUIDED READING ACTIVITY 8-3

1. islands
2. twenty
3. Osaka
4. Kyoto
5. clans
6. Yamato
7. Shotoku Taishi
8. government
9. centralized
10. Fujiwara
11. capital
12. "son of Heaven"
13. decentralized
14. aristocrats
15. samurai
16. Shinto
17. divinity
18. Japanese nation
19. code of behavior
20. China and Japan
21. East Asia
22. Koryo

GUIDED READING ACTIVITY 8-4

I. Buddhism
  A. Theravada
  B. Nirvana
II. Islam
  A. fought
  B. Turkish
III. Caspian Sea
  A. death
  B. sixteenth century
    1. the Moguls
    2. Portuguese
IV. foreign conquerors
  A. strict separation
  B. tolerant
  C. suspicion and dislike
V. architects
  A. Khajuraho
  B. Sanskrit prose

GUIDED READING ACTIVITY 8-5

1. geographical; mainland; islands
2. river valleys, mountain ranges; unified
3. Vietnamese; identity
4. Cambodia; Thai
5. frontier, China; capital
6. highlands; pastoral
7. Indian Ocean; Islam
8. states; northern India

VOCABULARY ACTIVITY 9

1. B
2. L
3. K
4. N
5. M
6. A

Answer Key

7. O

8. G

9. E

10. D

11. H

12. I

13. J

14. C

15. F

SKILLS REINFORCEMENT ACTIVITY 9

1. It represents an opinion. The expression "woman behind the man" implies that Theodora was responsible for her husband's success.

2. **a.** Justinian was well-educated. Theodora had been an actress before they were married. She gave jobs to friends. Justinian issued decrees allowing women to own land. There was a rebellion, which Justinian suppressed.

   b. They can be proved by looking in history books or an encyclopedia.

3. surprising, generously, fair, greatest

4. Theodora was a smart woman who was a good influence upon her husband, helping him to remain in power.

CRITICAL THINKING ACTIVITY 9

1. Answers will vary. Possible questions: What crops did Slav farmers plant? Did they plant only their own food, or did they grow large amounts of crops to sell and trade? Did they own their farms, or were they tenants? If they were tenants, who were the owners? Where did the owners live? Did farmers hire help? Whom did they hire? Did all family members work on the farms?

2. Answers will vary. Possible questions: How did the king treat his subjects and nobles? What powers had the king assumed? How did King John differ from his predecessor?

HISTORY AND GEOGRAPHY ACTIVITY 9

1. The availability of various resources, including food, clothing, shelter, and ways to make a living all influence the directions in which groups move.

2. Vikings sought new sources of land, wealth, and fame.

3. Initially, the Vikings sought to increase their wealth and access to foreign goods. The combination of Viking warrior tradition and the promise of new lands led Vikings to conquer and settle foreign lands.

4. Buried treasure points to various routes and patterns of movement during a particular period.

5. Students will need to do research to prepare for the debate. Encourage students to refer to their findings when debating to support their arguments.

MAPPING HISTORY ACTIVITY 9

1. about 850 miles

2. Black Sea; Mediterranean Sea

3. Arrows on map indicating the battle routes should point from Constantinople to Ad Decimum; from Ad Decimum to Sicily, Sardinia, and Corsica; from Sicily to Naples, Rome, and Ravenna; from Durres to Split; and from Cartagena into Spain.

HISTORICAL SIGNIFICANCE ACTIVITY 9

1. Vladivostok is a Russian city on the Pacific coast; Corfu is a Greek island in the Adriatic Sea.

2. **a.** Bartholomew I, patriarch of Constantinople, and the patriarchate of Moscow (Alexy)

Answer Key

b. Bartholomew I supports autonomy for the Estonian Orthodox parishes, but the patriarchate of Moscow wants control over them.

3. Rome, Italy, was the first Rome; the second "Rome" was Constantinople (now Istanbul); the third was Moscow.

COOPERATIVE LEARNING ACTIVITY 9

Students should complete the activity and answer the Group Process and Quick Check questions. Have students share their responses with their groups or with the class as a whole.

HISTORY SIMULATION ACTIVITY 9

Students should work collaboratively in groups toward achieving the learning objective of the History Simulation Activity.

TIME LINE ACTIVITY 9

1. 357

2. Otto I

3. William of Normandy

4. King John

5. 192 years

6. 1054

7. 10 years

8. Visigoths

LINKING PAST AND PRESENT ACTIVITY 9

1. As stated in the Magna Carta, the monarch was bound to consult his or her subjects on issues such as taxation. Meetings between the monarch and other people of prominence over important governmental affairs would gradually evolve into a more formal arrangement, the Parliament.

2. The members of the House of Commons are elected. Therefore, when a party wins a majority of seats in The House of Commons, its members can choose the prime minister. It also oversees the actions of the cabinet ministers.

3. Because the townspeople were wealthy, they may have been able to lend the monarch money. In return for royal favors, they may have been able to influence the poorer townspeople to take the monarch's side in disputes with powerful nobles. Students' reports should mention that the middle class gained power through establishing guilds and other trade organizations. They should discuss how the Crusades increased the importance of the middle class: As a result of the Crusades, towns became important trade centers; craftspeople made trade goods; and merchants extended their influence by forming business relationships with merchants from other countries. As global trade developed, merchants and other people of the commercial class became wealthier and more powerful than the nobles. They began to educate their children to become lawyers and church leaders.

PEOPLE IN WORLD HISTORY ACTIVITY 9, PROFILE 1

1. Theodora was an actress and the daughter of an animal trainer from Cyprus.

2. She persuaded Justinian to pass laws against wife beating, allow women to divorce their husbands, and permit women to own property and to keep their children if widowed.

3. Answers will vary. Possible answer: Nothing in the profile tells whether Theodora's influence was public or private. However, it is probably reasonable to infer that men generally disapproved of the new laws, whereas women approved.

PEOPLE IN WORLD HISTORY ACTIVITY 9, PROFILE 2

1. He converted to Eastern Orthodoxy from paganism.

Answer Key

2. They were required to convert as well. Churches were built, and the church gained important legal status.

3. to enjoy the advantages of an alliance with Byzantium

4. Answers will vary. Most students will say that it is unfair to force your religious beliefs on others. However, some students may support the principle of Christian conversion.

5. Answers will vary depending on research.

PRIMARY SOURCE READING 9

1. Initially, King Richard tried to use siege weaponry to bombard the city of Acre into surrender. He placed himself in the center of the battle and ordered a tunnel to be dug under the city's walls.

2. King Richard reasoned that people would fight bravely if they were paid extra to do so. Therefore, he promised gold coins for each brick of the city wall removed. This strategy inspired a large number of men to take many stones from the city's wall, in spite of great personal danger.

3. Saladin gave up 2,000 Christian nobles and 500 Christians of lesser ranks whom he was holding as hostages. He also promised that he and his army would leave the city with only the clothes they wore. In exchange for the release of Turkish prisoners, Saladin's forces paid Richard and the French king 200,000 talents. The kings demanded to hold prestigious Turks as security while the terms of the agreement were carried out.

4. Answers may vary. Students should back up their position (either in support of Saladin's surrender or in support of continued warfare against Richard and his allies) with material from the selection and a well-reasoned chain of logic.

5. The author of the selection seems to concentrate on the thoughts and emotions of the highest-ranking participants in the siege of Acre, notably King Richard, Saladin, and their respective advisers. It neglects the feelings and goals of the men doing the actual fighting, either the Turks defending the city or the Christians trying to take it.

RETEACHING ACTIVITY 9

1. Charlemagne becomes the Frankish king.

2. The Vikings begin to explore and conquer.

3. Gregory I becomes pope.

4. People turn to local nobles for protection.

5. William of Normandy is crowned king of England.

6. Magna Carta is signed.

7. Pope Urban II rallies Christians to liberate Jerusalem.

ENRICHMENT ACTIVITY 9

1. Answers may vary. Possible answer: Eastern Orthodox Populations in Several Countries

2. 10,647,511

3. Armenia, Greece

4. a. 4,351,737
   b. about 6 times
   c. about 11 percent

5. about 25 percent

6. about 6 million

WORLD ART AND MUSIC ACTIVITY 9

1. Hagia Sophia is a large rectangle. It has a square central room, with a half-circle room at either end. It has a large dome over the central square, and two half domes over the half-circle rooms.

2. The weight of the dome was transferred to supports in four places, so pillars and windows could be placed under the arches of the dome.

Answer Key

3. The inside was light and airy. It contained many pictures for people to look at. These pictures showed stories from the Bible or history that people knew.

4. Answers will vary. Students should note that the design of the arches enabled Hagia Sophia's designers to construct such a large dome. Additionally, the arches took the pressure off the supporting walls which allowed for the construction of windows and columns. Without the light admitted by these features, the church's interior world remain dark.

GUIDED READING ACTIVITY 9-1

1. A number of states ruled by German kings.

2. The Angles and Saxons, Germanic tribes from Denmark and northern Germany who moved into Britain at the beginning of the fifth century.

3. The kingdom of the Franks

4. His conversion gained him the support of the Roman Catholic Church.

5. The crucial social bond was family, especially the extended family of husbands, wives, children, brothers, sisters, cousins, and grandparents.

6. Wergild was the amount paid by a wrongdoer to the family of the person he or she had injured or killed.

7. The pope was the bishop, the highest ranking official of the church in the city of Rome, and claimed to be leader of the Roman Catholic Church.

8. Pope Gregory was especially active in converting the pagan peoples of Germanic Europe to Christianity.

9. The monks were the social workers of their communities, providing schools for the young, hospitality for travelers, and hospitals for the sick.

10. His coronation symbolized the coming together of the Roman, Christian, and Germanic elements that make up the basis of European civilization.

11. Because they were copied by Carolingian monks.

GUIDED READING ACTIVITY 9-2

1. True.

2. False. Far-reaching attacks came from the Northmen, also known as the Vikings.

3. False. The Frankish policy of converting the Vikings to Christianity was a deliberate one.

4. True.

5. False. Europe was dominated by heavily armored cavalry, or knights.

6. True.

7. True.

8. False. European society was dominated by men whose chief concern was warfare.

9. True.

10. True.

GUIDED READING ACTIVITY 9-3

1. Normandy

2. the Battle of Hastings

3. England

4. Normans

5. Anglo-Saxon

6. monarchy

7. Canterbury

8. Thomas à Becket

9. Runnymeade

10. Magna Carta

11. absolute

12. Parliament

13. Romans

Answer Key

14. Holy Roman Empire
15. Bohemian
16. Christianity
17. Viking
18. Mongols

GUIDED READING ACTIVITY 9-4

I. emperor
   A. codification
   B. imperial
II. Islam
   A. Yarmuk
   B. smaller
      1. Byzantine
      2. Christian, Eastern Orthodox Church
III. Macedonians
   A. split
   B. excommunicated
IV. Crusades
   A. western
   B. Jerusalem
   C. pilgrims
   D. attacks

VOCABULARY ACTIVITY 10

Across

1. *taille*
8. charter
9. journeyman
10. scholasticism
12. relic
13. master

Down

2. sacrament
3. apprentice
4. money economy
5. vernacular
6. troubadour

7. manor
11. interdict

SKILLS REINFORCEMENT ACTIVITY 10

1. the spread of the Black Death
2. 1347 to 1352
3. The map key shows the spread of the epidemic by year, the cities spared, and the cities seriously affected by the plague.
4. Cities seriously affected by the plague include Oxford, London, Amiens, Paris, Barcelona, Avignon, Genoa, Pisa, Venice, Florence, Siena, Messina, Vienna, Bremen, Lübeck, and Constantinople.

CRITICAL THINKING SKILLS ACTIVITY 10

1. The monk likes riding his horse and hunting.
2. The monk doesn't think much of the rules of his order and does not follow them. He likes the new, modern world.
3. He wears expensive clothes with fur and gold and has many fine horses and fast greyhounds.
4. A reformer might object to the monk's behavior and appearance because he is obviously concerned with worldly goods, such as his appearance and property, rather than religion. His monastery seems to be fairly wealthy. He should be looking after the poor and the sick and be carrying out his religious duties rather than hunting and riding all over the countryside.

HISTORY AND GEOGRAPHY ACTIVITY 10

1. Technology presents new ideas and strategies for change, which can offer opportunities for progress.
2. Advances in agriculture, urban planning, environmental planning, and space technology may all have an impact on physical environments.

Answer Key

3. The significance of the Church and the Christian religion in medieval life called for splendid structures to reflect that importance.

4. Students might compare the ability to build a very tall masonry building to building skyscrapers or underground cities.

5. Emphasize to students that they will have to suspend their knowledge of what is possible today and concentrate on how their community has changed over the years. You might want to arrange a visit to the local historical society, if possible, as part of their project.

MAPPING HISTORY ACTIVITY 10

1. large areas in the southwest and two small areas in the north

2. a large area in the north and west, a narrow strip through the center, and a large area in the southeast

3. Agincourt, Crécy, Orléans

4. Reims should be marked just above the C in Champagne. Students' routes should connect Orléans, Reims, and Calais.

HISTORICAL SIGNIFICANCE ACTIVITY 10

Location:
Middle Ages: London on the river bank, in a public cook shop; *Today:* in shops, on street corners, in malls

Foods:
Middle Ages: various meats, fish, and birds; *Today:* hamburgers, chicken, French fries, pizza

Customers:
Middle Ages: rich and poor, soldiers, travelers; *Today:* rich and poor, travelers, teenagers, families

Reasons for Purchasing:
Middle Ages: too tired to cook, impatient for food, traveling; *Today:* too tired to cook, impatient for food, traveling, as snack or treat

COOPERATIVE LEARNING ACTIVITY 10

Students should complete the activity and answer the Group Process and Quick Check questions. Have students share their responses with their groups or with the class as a whole.

HISTORY SIMULATION ACTIVITY 10

Students should work collaboratively in groups toward achieving the learning objective of the History Simulation Activity.

TIME LINE ACTIVITY 10

1. universities

2. 72 years

3. the Hundred Years' War

4. 19 years old

5. Battle of Crécy and Battle of Agincourt

6. thirteenth century

7. War of the Roses

LINKING PAST AND PRESENT ACTIVITY 10

1. In the Middle Ages, the sources of money for poor relief were more diversified. Money came from private individuals, guilds, religious organizations, private individuals, and town or city governments. Today, although religious and private organizations provide some help, national governments provide most of the money for poverty relief and social services by taxing their citizens.

2. It keeps the crime and disease rates down, helps create a more peaceful and harmonious social environment, and promotes a sense of humane behavior between people.

3. Medieval leaders feared that the poor might rebel against the local governments and engage in crime. Students' reports should include information on such punishments as execution, whipping, and branding. They should recognize that harsh punishments, especially death, for

Answer Key

minor crimes led people to commit greater acts of violence, since they had little to lose by doing so.

PEOPLE IN WORLD HISTORY ACTIVITY 10, PROFILE 1

1. France and England

2. She grew up in an atmosphere of poetry, literature, and music, and was educated in two languages.

3. Answers will vary, but should include her being queen of both France and England, and being an educated and powerful woman.

PEOPLE IN WORLD HISTORY ACTIVITY 10, PROFILE 2

1. to unify Spain under a strong monarchy

2. Answers may include conquering the Moors and expanding her territory, standardizing coinage, codifying laws, building roads, and sponsoring Christopher Columbus.

3. Answers will vary. Possible answers: her persecution of Jews, the creation of the Spanish Inquisition, and her warfare against the Moors.

4. Students may say that a true conversion of faith cannot be forced. During Isabella's reign, Jews converted in order to escape expulsion or execution.

PRIMARY SOURCE READING 10

1. The fourteenth-century author of the *Decameron*.

2. To explain the social context of his story.

3. People feared exposure to the disease; for many, the focus of life was survival.

4. Some people avoided contact with others, while others practiced moderation; some people sought only pleasure and practiced a hedonistic lifestyle.

RETEACHING ACTIVITY 10

Answers will vary but may include the following examples:

Economics: manorial system; Europe's economy begins to revive; trade among towns increases; rise of money economy; organization of guilds; Hundred Years' War strains economy

Religion: Joan of Arc condemned as a heretic; the Great Schism; Jan Hus; Cistercians; the Franciscans were founded by Saint Francis of Assisi; Dominican order battles heresy; veneration of saints

Education: growth of towns creates need for officials and lawyers; universities begin; learning increases; Thomas Aquinas

Military: battles of Crécy and Agincourt; Joan of Arc leads French forces to Orléans; War of the Roses; 1492, Muslims and Jews forced out of Spain

Arts: universities and learning lead to changes in artistic production; chansons de geste; *Song of Roland*; use of vernacular increases

ENRICHMENT ACTIVITY 10

1. Answers may vary. Students may find they have too many tasks for one day. Encourage them to think of management procedures and time allocation (doing certain tasks every day and some only on certain days) to complete as many tasks as possible. They should discover that managing a household was complicated and required good management skills.

2. Lists and locations will vary. Help students to think of the various locations within a castle and its grounds where they might have gathered foods for their meal. Remind them that travel around the estate and to marketplaces was time-consuming and often difficult.

WORLD ART AND MUSIC ACTIVITY 10

1. Troubadours were wandering poet-musicians.

Answer Key

2. Their songs were usually about love for an unattainable woman.

3. Answers will vary. Possible answers: Women were revered to the point that they were considered goddesses or angels, not human beings. They should be adored but not possessed.

4. Answers will vary. Possible answer: Yes. The first song talks about love, and since the poet keeps pleading with the woman, it seems that she is resisting. The second song consists of a dialogue in which a young man seeks advice from his king about love. Both songs describe love as an anguished experience because women are unattainable.

GUIDED READING ACTIVITY 10-1

1. The number of people almost doubled from 38 million to 74 million people.

2. Conditions in Europe were more settled and peaceful after the invasions of the early Middle Ages had stopped. Food production increased because a change in climate improved growing conditions.

3. A new horse collar and the use of the horseshoe.

4. A manor was an agricultural estate run by a lord and worked by peasants.

5. By giving the lords a share of every product they raised, paying for the use of common pasture lands and turning over a part of the catch from ponds or streams.

6. Christmas (celebrating the birth of Christ), Easter (celebrating the resurrection of Christ), and Pentecost (celebrating the descent of the Holy Spirit on Christ's disciples 50 days after His resurrection).

7. A revival of trade and an associated growth of towns and cities.

8. Because it was located along a trade route and because the lords of the castle would offer protection.

9. The right to buy and sell property, freedom from military service to the lord, a law guaranteeing the freedom of the townspeople, and the right for an escaped serf to become a free person after living a year and a day in the town.

10. The cities were dirty and smelled from animal and human waste. Air was polluted from wood fires. Water was polluted as well.

11. He first became an apprentice to a master craftsperson. After 5–7 years he became a journeyman and worked for wages. Upon completing a masterpiece which was judged, he/she could be declared a master and join a guild.

GUIDED READING ACTIVITY 10-2

1. True.

2. False. These objects symbolized the spiritual authority that the official was granted by the church.

3. True.

4. False. An interdict forbids priests from giving the sacraments to a specific group.

5. False. Both men and women joined religious orders in increasing numbers.

6. True.

7. True.

8. False. He was led to abandon all worldly goods and to live and preach in poverty.

9. False. The Church's desire to have a method of discovering and dealing with heretics led to the Inquisition.

10. True.

11. False. They believed a pilgrimage to a holy shrine produced a spiritual benefit.

GUIDED READING ACTIVITY 10-3

I. university
   A. European
   B. lecture

Answer Key

1. exams

2. law, medicine, theology

II. Scholasticism

  A. Christian, Greek

  B. Reconcile; reason, experience

III. Vernacular

  A. troubadour

  B. battles, political

IV. Romanesque

  A. pillars, walls

  B. Gothic

    1. vaults, arches

    2. buttress

  C. stained glass

GUIDED READING ACTIVITY 10-4

1. natural

2. rats; fleas

3. 38 million

4. Jews, poisoning

5. declined, suffered

6. taxed

7. Frenchman

8. John Hus

9. Hundred Years' War

10. Peasant

11. resources

12. saints

13. cannon, gunpowder

14. King Louis XI

15. War of the Roses

16. Jews, Muslims

17. independently

18. centralize

19. Mongols

VOCABULARY ACTIVITY 11

1. C

2. E

3. A

4. G

5. I

6. B

7. H

8. J

9. D

10. F

11. Paragraphs will vary but should include at least five of the terms.

SKILLS REINFORCEMENT ACTIVITY 11

1. Primary sources: the journal of Pedro de Castañeda, 1560; *Royal Commentaries of the Incas*, by Garcilaso de la Vega, 1600s. Secondary Sources: *Aztecs: An Interpretation* by Inga Clendinnen, 1991; *Civilizations in the West* by Mark Kishlansky, Patrick Geary, and Patricia O'Brien, 1991

2. Inga Clendinnen, Mark Kishlansky, Patrick Geary, and Patricia O'Brien are modern historians. Pedro de Castañeda was a soldier in the army of Francisco Coronado. Garcilaso de la Vega was born in Peru in 1539 of Inca and Spanish ancestry.

3. No, because it is possible that a translator may misinterpret a statement in a document or distort what the original author had in mind when he or she originally wrote the piece.

CRITICAL THINKING SKILLS ACTIVITY 11

1. Possible questions: What events in the life of Pacal might the hieroglyphs describe? Could the hieroglyphs have given clues to

Answer Key

the reasons for the end of the Mayan civilization? How did Palenque architecture reflect daily Mayan life?

2. Answers will depend on students' activities and research interests. Questions should provide a basis for focusing research.

HISTORY AND GEOGRAPHY ACTIVITY 11

1. Climate, soil, landforms, and other physical features affect the natural vegetation and animal life of a region as well as which crops can be cultivated.

2. People may irrigate land in order to grow food, they may remove naturally occurring vegetation such as trees or grasses in order to grow crops, and their crops may change the quality of the soil. Removal of forest or grasslands will affect the animals found in a region. People might also build roads or trails to facilitate trade.

3. Farming is a stationary practice, so people were able to survive in one place. Bison moved from place to place, so people who lived on bison had to follow them.

4. The types of dwellings people build, the types of clothing they wear, and the kinds of symbols used in their religion are all examples of aspects of culture that could be affected by geography.

5. A people's history, trading partners, personality of leaders, and technology are all examples of other things that can affect culture.

6. Results will vary but should provide information about Native Americans who lived in the area and how the geography and natural resources affected their diet and dwellings. If the people lived in permanent settlements, they changed the environment by building structures; if farmers, they changed it by removing some vegetation. If they were hunter-gatherer bands, they may not have changed the geography.

MAPPING HISTORY ACTIVITY 11

1. to Chaco Canyon

2. Zape to Rio Grande Pueblos

3. Students' drawings should clearly distinguish the routes of the Cholula from that of the Teotihuacán and Tula. Lines should appear from Cholula to the **X** on the west coast, the **Y** on the east coast, Casas Grandes to "Hohokam," and Casas Grandes to "Hopi."

HISTORICAL SIGNIFICANCE ACTIVITY 11

1. sources of food and water, materials for building shelter

2. Water pollution threatens fishing sites. Pollution of land and water threaten farmlands and animals that are hunted.

3. Answers will vary. Students may suggest that leaders accept an industry because of fees that the industry pays to the tribe, or because of the jobs that an industry creates.

4. Students may suggest that if tribal sovereignty continues to hold high standards, reservation land will be the only environmentally safe land left in the country.

COOPERATIVE LEARNING ACTIVITY 11

Students should complete the activity and answer the Group Process and Quick Check questions. Have students share their responses with their groups or with the class as a whole.

HISTORY SIMULATION ACTIVITY 11

Students should work collaboratively in groups toward achieving the learning objective of the History Simulation Activity.

TIME LINE ACTIVITY 11

1. 7

2. Olmec, Teotihuacán, Toltec, Anasazi

Answer Key

3. They lived in different areas of Mesoamerica.

4. It was the earliest known civilization of Mesoamerica.

5. The only assumption one could make is that the two civilizations had some contact. Although the Maya began before the Toltec, they overlapped in time. Therefore, it would be unclear whether the design originated with the Toltec or the Maya.

LINKING PAST AND PRESENT ACTIVITY 11

1. The slash-and-burn technique for clearing farm fields is common to both groups. After clearing a field, the Maya let it lie fallow for four to seven years to prepare it for use. Modern agriculturists use a field right away, often destroying it in several years. In addition, modern farmers use chemicals that eventually damage the water and soil.

2. Since plant roots suck water from the underlying lake, the *chinampas* probably wouldn't need watering. The plants might eventually transform the shallow lake into a drier area by sucking up its water and trapping more soil with its roots.

3. Rain forests manufacture oxygen, take carbon dioxide from the atmosphere, and by exuding and trapping moisture, prevent droughts. Rain forests also support a large number of animal and plant species. Students' reports should explain that all living things play important roles in keeping ecological systems healthy. Students' reports should also point out that tropical plants and animals can provide useful things such as medicine and that some undiscovered plants might possess the cures for serious diseases.

PEOPLE IN WORLD HISTORY ACTIVITY 11, PROFILE 1

1. When he died, some of his followers were so loyal that they committed suicide, and the city mourned his death for a year.

2. He planned for future famines and made sure there was enough food to feed the populace.

3. Answers will vary, but might include Topa Inca's ability to expand the empire without using any of his father's acquired wealth.

PEOPLE IN WORLD HISTORY ACTIVITY 11 PROFILE 2

1. All children, even those of enslaved persons, were born free.

2. Answers may vary, but should refer to the alliance made with Texcoco and the destruction of Azcapotzalco.

3. Answers will vary. Students may suggest that while the destruction of Azcapotzalco supports the conquistador's comments, his comments are also exaggerations that support his own position as part of an invading force. Itzcoatl's descendants might describe the conquistadors as equally fierce and cruel.

PRIMARY SOURCE READING ACTIVITY 11

1. Raven can assume different forms (such as that of the old man), remove and replace body parts, and swim underwater.

2. The young chief is determined that future Ah-wah-nee children will always remember the proud and brave blood that flowed in the veins of their ancestors.

3. They cheer their admiration for their great chief and rename him Chief Yo Semitee, which means "Grizzly Bear."

4. Raven is a trickster who likes to confound people with his cleverness.

Answer Key

5. To be a chief, he must prove his bravery in spectacular ways.

RETEACHING ACTIVITY 11

Northern North America: Inuit, Iroquois, Mound Builders, Anasazi, Plains Indians
Mesoamerica: Maya, Olmec, Aztec, Toltec
South America: Inca, Moche

ENRICHMENT ACTIVITY 11

1. They thought that history recurred in cyclical patterns and that by understanding these patterns they could create a favorable destiny.

2. Possible answers: to interpret Mayan history in a way that we can understand today yet is true to the Maya's perceptions of themselves; to reveal the humanity of the Maya.

3. The written history of the Americas begins then with the written records left by the Maya.

4. Students who answer yes may argue that the Maya contributed to the civilizations that created modern Mexico and Central America. Students who argue no may claim that due to the settlement of the Americas by Europeans and the destruction of indigenous cultures, the Mayan way of thought has had little lasting impact on the Americas.

WORLD ART AND MUSIC ACTIVITY 11

1. Cedar trees were hollowed out. Then animals (and sometimes people) were carved in the wood. When the carving was completed, the poles would be painted bright colors.

2. to give information about its owners, to commemorate special events, to honor the dead, and to mark graves

3. Answers will vary. Possible answer: Native Americans believe that animals have special powers and responsibilities for humankind. Animals help, protect, and guide humans.

4. Answers will vary. Possible answers: Based on the fact that the figure is holding two fish, the totem pole may have contained guardian spirits that provided for prosperous fishing. It also may have represented a skilled fisher.

GUIDED READING ACTIVITY 11-1

1. From the Arctic Ocean in the north to Cape Horn at the tip of South America

2. Between 100,000 and 8,000 years ago, the last Ice Age produced low sea levels that created this land bridge.

3. The Inuit had to learn unique ways to survive in such a cold and harsh environment.

4. They are best known for the elaborate earth mounds that they built.

5. The Iroquois lived in villages that consisted of longhouses surrounded by a wooden fence for protection.

6. Iroquois men hunted and protected the community. Women prepared meals, made baskets and took care of the children.

7. A council of representatives (a group of 50 Iroquois leaders) known as the Grand Council met regularly to settle differences among league members.

8. The men left their villages to hunt buffalo, a very important animal to the Plains culture.

9. The Anasazi used canals and earthen dams to turn parts of the desert into fertile gardens. They were skilled at making baskets and beautifully crafted pottery. They used stone and adobe to build pueblos.

10. A pueblo was a multi-storied structure that could house many people.

Answer Key

GUIDED READING ACTIVITY 11-2

1. False. Mesoamerica is a name we use for areas of Mexico and Central America that were civilized before the Spaniards arrived.

2. True.

3. False. The Maya built splendid temples and pyramids and even developed a complicated calendar.

4. True.

5. False. Rulers of the Mayan city-states claimed to be descended from the gods.

6. False. The name of the supreme god of the Mayans was Itzamna (Lizard House).

7. True.

8. True.

9. False. The Toltec were a fierce and warlike people who extended their conquests into Mayan lands.

10. True.

11. False. The Aztec thought that representatives of the god Quetzalcoatl had returned.

GUIDED READING ACTIVITY 11-3

1. Caral
2. Western Hemisphere
3. Supe
4. Moche

5. 1000 B.C.
6. Inca
7. southern
8. Pachacuti
9. war
10. army
11. wheel
12. llamas
13. roads
14. Colombia
15. Santiago, Chile
16. suspension
17. ravines and waterways
18. buildings and monuments
19. European
20. architectural
21. Machu Picchu
22. knotted strings
23. *quipu*
24. diseases
25. smallpox
26. emperor
27. Pizzaro
28. Lima

ACKNOWLEDGMENTS

TEXT

9 "The Story of the Merchant and the Demon" from *The Arabian Nights: The Thousand and One Nights* by Husain Haddawy. Copyright © 1990 by W.W. Norton. Reprinted by permission of W.W. Norton & Company, Inc.

11 "The Fisherman and the Jinnee" from *Tales from the Thousand and One Nights* translated by N.J. Dawood (Penguin Classics 1954, revised edition 1973). Translation copyright © 1954, 1973 by N.J. Dawood.

18 From *Season of Migration to the North* by Tayeb Salih, translated by Denys Johnson-Davies, copyright © 1969 by Tayeb Salih and Denys Johnson-Davies.

31 *From The Arabs: Their Heritage and Their Way of Life* by Rhoda Hoff. Copyright © 1979 by Rhoda Hoff Detera. Reprinted by permission of David McKay Co., a division of Random House, Inc.

59 From *The East African Coast*, G.S.P. Freeman-Grenville. © 1962 Oxford University Press. Reprinted by permission.

85 "Digha Nikaya" from *Sources of Indian Tradition* edited by Wm. Theodore de Bary. Copyright © 1964 by Columbia University Press. Reprinted with permission of the publisher.

113 From "The Siege and Capture of Acre" translated by James A. Brundage, Ph.D., from *Crusades: A Documentary Survey* by James A. Brundage, Ph.D. Copyright © 1962 by The Marquette University Press.

128 From *The Canterbury Tales* by Geoffrey Chaucer, translated by David Wright, translation copyright © 1985 by David Wright.

141 From "The Black Death, 1348," EyeWitness—history through the eyes of those who lived it, www.ibis.com. Copyright © 2001, Ibis Communications, Inc. Reprinted by permission.

146 "Will you love me" and "King Theobald, Sire, advise me" from *Music of the Middle Ages I* by Giulio Cattin translated by Steven Botterill, copyright © 1984 by Cambridge University Press.

155 From *Aztecs: An Interpretation*, by Inga Clendinnen, copyright © 1991 by Cambridge University Press.

From *Royal Commentaries of the Incas*, Part One, by Carcilaso de la Vega, El Inca, tr. by Harold V. Livermore, copyright © 1966 by University of Texas Press.

From *Riding With Coronado*, adapted and edited by Robert Meredith and Edric B. Smith, Jr., copyright © 1964 by Edric B. Smith, Jr. and Robert K. Meredith. By permission of Little, Brown and Company.

From *Civilizations in the West*, by Mark Kishlansky, Patrick Geary, and Patricia O'Brien, copyright © 1991 by Harper Collins Publishers.

157 From "American Food Crops in the Old World" by William H. McNeill from *Seeds of Change: A Quincentennial Commemoration* edited by Herman J. Viola and Carolyn Margolis, copyright © 1991 by the Smithsonian Institution.

169 From *Voices of the Winds* by Margot Edmonds & Ella Clark. Copyright © 1989 by Margot Edmonds & Ella E. Clark. Reprinted by permission of Facts On File, Inc., NY.

PHOTOGRAPHS

19 Robert Azzi/Woodfin Camp

29 Reproduced by kind permission of the Trustees of the Chester Beatty Library, Dublin

30 The Art Archive

35 AKG, Berlin/SuperStock

ACKNOWLEDGMENTS

57 Werner Forman Archive/Art Resource, NY

58 Bibliothèque Nationale, Paris

63 The Metropolitan Museum of Art, The Michael C. Rockefeller Collection, Gift of Nelson A. Rockefeller, 1972 (1978.412.310)

83 Asian Art & Archaeology, Inc./CORBIS

84 Asian Art Archives of the University of Michigan

89 Laurie Platt Winfrey, Inc.

111 Scala/Art Resource, NY

112 Private Collection/The Bridgeman Art Library

117 SuperStock

139 Mary Evans Picture Library

140 AKG Photo

145 Ronald Sheridan/Ancient Art & Architecture Collection

167 Stock Montage, Inc.

168 Pasztory, Esther, *Aztec Art*, Harry N. Abrams, Inc., Publishers, 1983

173 J. Warden/SuperStock

Teacher Notes

Teacher Notes